AUM HINDUTVAM

[*Daily Religious Rites of the Hindus*]

SWAMI VEDANANDA

MOTILAL BANARSIDASS PUBLISHERS
PRIVATE LIMITED • DELHI

Revised and Enlarged Edition: *Delhi, 1993*

ISBN: 81-208-1081-3

Also available at:
MOTILAL BANARSIDASS
41 U.A., Bungalow Road, Jawahar Nagar, Delhi 110 007
120 Royapettah High Road, Mylapore, Madras 600 004
16 St. Mark's Road, Bangalore 560 001
Ashok Rajpath, Patna 800 004
Chowk, Varanasi 221 001

PRINTED IN INDIA
BY JAINENDRA PRAKASH JAIN AT SHRI JAINENDRA PRESS, A-45 NARAINA INDUSTRIAL AREA, PHASE I, NEW DELHI 110028 AND PUBLISHED BY NARENDRA PRAKASH JAIN FOR MOTILAL BANARSIDASS PUBLISHERS PVT. LTD., BUNGALOW ROAD, JAWAHAR NAGAR, DELHI 110 007

THE DIVINE NATION-BUILDER

During the nineteenth and the first part of the twentieth century, a galaxy of religious prophets, social reformers, cultural magnets and nation-builders appeared successively in Indian national life. Acharyya Swami Pranavanandaji is the last and greatest of them. Acharyya's nation-building movement has included all the previous ones—spiritual, moral, religious, educational, social and cultural.

Bharat Sevasram Sangha, a spiritual brotherhood of sannyasins and selfless workers, organised by this great patriot-saint, has pushed on its activities in all the spheres of the social and national life of India—individual, as well as collective.

A few words about the life and character of the Divine personality is being given here to enable the public to understand the fountain of inspiration whence the Bharat Sevasram Sangha has been drawing its uninterrupted life-energy.

The Acharyya is held as an incarnation of Lord Shiva, the God of gods. The fact is that his father was a great devotee of Shiva. Confronted by a series of dangers and difficulties, due to the conspiracy of a local zamindar and finding no other means to extricate himself, he undertook a year-long penance of propitiating Shiva by meditations and prayers throughout the whole night; which moved the great God to pity. Lord Shiva vouchsafed to incarnate Himself as his son. Soon after this, a son was born to Sri Bishnu Charan Das on the auspicious day of Maghipurnima in the year 1896 A.D.

The boy was a prodigy from his very childhood. Unlike other boys, he seldom communicated with the world outside. Having no desire for food or merry-making, he remained immersed in deep meditation and self-contemplation. He used to take a few handfuls of rice and a few boiled potatoes for his daily diet and carefully shunned all rich and palatable dishes. But with this scanty diet he used to take heavy physical exercise with a pair of huge clubs, as a result of which he acquired uncommon physical strength. As the boy grew older he meditated deeply on the transitoriness of the world and on the frailties and futilities of mundane life and exerted himself heart and soul to realise the Ultimate Truth and the means of Deliverance. His continuous meditation, sharp discrimination and total dispassion reminded people of the lives of two other great prophets, Lord Buddha and Acharyya Shankara, and also of the fact that he was an incarnation of Lord Shiva. The Acharyya was named Binode in his childhood. Binode could scarcely pay attention to his studies.

During the first part of his life of spiritual austerities, he would occasionally attend to the surrounding boys and youths and help them to build up their spiritual life and moral character. Later on, after his spiritual initiation by Yogiraj Gambhirnath-ji, he became totally lost to the world. Intoxicated with the beatitude of Realisation in the Super-conscious state for the next few years till 1916, he attained Divine Illumination on the auspicious Maghi Purnima Day and founded the illustrious Bharat Sevasram Sangha.

Hundreds of selfless youths gradually rallied to this Divine Acharyya in connection with various activities—humanitarian, spiritual, moral, educational, religious and social—rapidly growing in number and magnitude. The Acharyya shaped, after those of his own, the life and character of these enthusiastic youngsters, who renounced the world and dedicated themselves to the service of the Sangha. Realisation of Self and service to humanity as Self, embodied, was the aim and object of the young disciples.

With this sacrificing, devoted and trained band of workers, the Acharyya chalked out a plan of nation-building activities and pushed the same on to the entire rank and file of the society. He himself guided with his spiritual vision and Divine intuition his organisation for over twenty years and laid down his life as Divine Martyr in harness.

CONTENTS

AUM

HINDUTVAM

RESURRECTION OF THE HINDUS

यदा यदा हि धर्मस्य ग्लानिर्भवति भारत
अभ्युत्थानमधर्मस्य तदात्मानं सृजाम्यहम् ।।
परित्राणाय साधूनां विनाशाय च दुष्कृताम्
धर्मसंस्थापनार्थाय संभवामि युगे युगे ।।

(गीता ४/८)

yadā yadā hi dharmasya glānirbhavati bhārata
abhyutthānamadharmasya tadātmānaṁ sṛjāmyaham ||
paritrāṇāya sādhūnāṁ vināśāya ca duṣkṛtām
dharmasaṁsthāpanārthāya saṁbhavāmi yuge yuge ||

"O Bharata! Whenever virtue declines and vice prevails, I incarnate myself. I appear, epoch after epoch, to save the virtuous, to eradicate the sinners, and to establish Law and Order."

The message of Lord Krishna came true in different ages, on different occasions, and with different people, in the past. Again, the situation has called forth the great Saviour, who has appeared in our midst as the Jugacharya—Shrimat Swami Pranavanandaji, the great Saviour of our age—the Divine Light, to guide our steps and check the erring. His clarion call is being heard. The Hindus have been aroused from their deep slumber of thousands of years and, armed with strong determination, have set out in their victorious march on the path of progress, shattering into pieces the impregnable facade of inactivity, impotency, cowardice, weariness, and despair. Who is there on the face of the earth that dares to stand against this resurrection?

The Samanvaya Movement or Synthetic Re-adjustment of the Hindu Society

At the instance of Jugacharya, the great saviour of the age, the movement for a synthetic re-adjustment of the Hindu Society has been gaining ground with electric speed throughout the length and breadth of the civilised world. The movement has been attracting every Hindu, of every rank, from the highly educated and cultured to the most uneducated, uncultured, uncared—for and ignored, towards the ever—peaceful and warm embrace of the gracious Jugacharya. Batches of selfless Sannyasins, re-infused with the Divine Spirit of Jugacharya and fully trained according to his ideal, are approaching every hearth and home, throughout India and abroad, with the great message of Hindu cultural regeneration.

Milan Mandir or Centre of Unity

With a view to achieving Hindu re-generation through synthetic social re-adjustment, innumerable HINDU MILAN MANDIRS or Centres of Hindu Unity have been established, so as to unite the scattered and disintegrated Hindu masses and to induce them to cultivate thoughts and practices conducive to religious and social welfare. In Hindu Milan Mandirs, highly educated and cultured Hindus have joined hands with the so-called uncultured, lowly people in society. Bound up with brotherly love and affection, they are devoting themselves whole-heartedly to the realization of the ideal. Every Hindu, whatever his social rank and status, has equal rights and privileges with every other Hindu. There is no place for division and distinction between the high and the low, the educated and the uneducated, the touchable and the untouchable. Mutual affection and regard, friendship and co-operation, sympathy and fellow-feeling reig in every Hindu Milan Mandir. Unity and solidarity of the Hindus of all ranks is being achieved, through a common bond of common ideal and purpose. Through the activities of these Hindu Milan Mandirs, attempts are being made to solve the problems arising from the removal of untouchability, reconversion of the renegades, stopping further conversion, and so on. Jugacharya himself gave the start to the organisation of one, united, Great Hindu Nation, by calling up every Hindu from every nook and corner, by marking him with the insignia of unity, by whispering into his ears the message of hope and courage, and embracing him with Divine love and affection.

Unite Under the Banner of Jugacharya

O ambitious Hindu! Arise! Awake!—muster strong under the banner of the greatest Unity and Divine Love, hoisted by Jugacharya himself, and proceed on with rapturous delight, in your victorious march towards regeneration. The tide has turned—the delusion and self-forgetfulness of thousands of years are being dispelled the re-wakening and the revival are stimulating every nerve of the Hindu society; the yearning and determination for self-preservation and self-defence are getting keener and keener; the eagerness for self-development and self-expansion has infused a new life in the Hindu society and made it fully active. Above all, Jugacharya, inspired by Mahashakti, the Divine Mother and the emblem of Primal Energy, is himself the helmsman. Do not look back, do not neglect, do not miss the surest golden opportunity. Arise! Awake!

Vedas: The Sanctuary of Hindu Religion and Nationality

According to Hindu religion, views regarding the modes and pathways of religions practice are multiple. The Vedas are the source of all of them—the mainspring. They are approachable only through samadhi or pure intuition and meditation. They are revealed texts, most fundamental, ultimate and infallible.

The real unity and synthesis of innumerable sects and branches of the Hindu society lie in the methods of Vedic prayer, Vedic rituals and their practices. The real basis or a common platform, whereupon the vast masses of the scattered, far-flung and disintegrated Hindu public may most conveniently unite, is but the universal, eternal, supreme, and deep-seated truths of the Vedas.

The Vedas are the Basis of Synthetic Re-adjustment

A study of the past history of Hindu religion and society shows that, whoever appeared as an Acharya in whatever epoch, with a view to uniting the scattered and disintegrated Hindu masses and establishing law and order by eradicating religious degradations and dissipations, accepted the Vedas as the ultimate basis of re-organisation and re-adjustment. Bhagvat Geeta—the Divine nectar-message of Lord Krishna, which was meant for spiritual revival and nation-building purposes, is essentially a synthesis of the Vedas, i.e. Upanishads.

Thus, it was said—

"...सर्वोपनिषदो गावो दोग्धा गोपालनन्दनः ...".

That is, "All the Upanishads are as cows and Lord Krishna is one who milks... "

The monistic interpretation of the Vedanta and the Upanishads formed the basis of religious revival and social re-organisation of the Hindus, as brought about by Acharya Sankara. The Indian nation-building scheme of Swami Vivekananda is also based on the Vedanta philosophy. The religious views of the different religious sects, as established by the different Acharyas like Madhvacharya, Nimbarkacharya, Vallabhacharya, Ramanujacharya, and Sri Sri Chaitanya Deva, are all but different interpretations of the Vedanta, suited to their respective time and situation. The Brahmo Samaj, as established by Raja Rammohun Roy and the Arya Samaj, as organised by Swami Dayananda, are both based respectively upon Brahma Veda (Monistic conception) of the Tantras and Upanishads and Prayer and the Jnanakanda (the chapter on knowledge) of the Vedas. Buddhism and Jainism, as promulgated by Buddha Deva and Mahavira respectively, are not anti-Vedic. The Karmakanda (the chapter on rituals) may be abandoned but how can Upasanakanda (chapter on prayer) and Jnanakanda (chapter on knowledge) be forsaken?

Jugacharya Swami Pranavanandaji, the renowned social reformer, has been determined to re-organise the Hindu masses into one undivided, compact Hindu society, through the preaching and teaching of Vedic ideals, rituals, prayers and practices, and has thus accepted the Vedas, as the basis of the great synthesis.

Abandon Anti-Vedic Views and Rituals

In course of hundreds and hundreds of years, because of political and social revolutions and contact with foreign nations and religions, Hindus have become accustomed to innumerable anti-Vedic tendencies and ideals, which have entered into the religious practices and social customs of their society. As a consequence, those very anti-Vedic tendencies and rituals are now being encouraged and observed by them, as if they are approved by the Hindu scriptures. In the clear sunlight of the life-ideal and realization of the Jugacharya, everything that is foreign and anti-Vedic, is to be analysed and critically seen through and abandoned.

Throw off the Shackles Imposed Upon by the Meaningless and Stereotyped Customs, Usages and Female Conventions in Vogue

In course of centuries of foreign dominations, the Hindu society, badly hit by multifarious untoward circumstances and destructive revolutionary movements, and absolutely bedevilled in matters of self-defence, was crowded with various customs, meaningless and harmful conventions, and female usages. Due to prolonged habit and practice of those pernicious and anti-Vedic customs and usages, the Hindu society has forgotten the Vedic truth, ideals, and rituals, and has been devoting itself to the observance of anti-Vedic and foreign practices. Thus, the Hindu society is split up into various sections with distinctions and mutual jealousy, animosity and hatred.

O Hindus! With your aim at national solidarity, stand upon the high altitude of Hinduism; give up the meaningless anti-Vedic customs, usages, and female conventions; take shelter under the banner of Vedic ideals, assemble and unite and offer your prayers as follows:

"ओं सह नाववतु सह नौ भुनक्तु सह वीर्यं करवावहै ।"

Oṁ saha nāvavatu saha nau bhunaktu, saha vīryaṁ karavāvahai |

"Save us jointly, rear us jointly, unite and strengthen us."

Every Hindu has a Right to the Study of the Vedas

God in the form of the Vedas, proclaimed to the whole human world—

यथेमां वाचं कल्याणीमावदानि जनेभ्यः।
ब्रह्मराजन्याभ्यां शूद्राय चार्याय च स्वाय चारणाय ॥

yathemāṁ vācaṁ kalyāṇīmāvadāni janebhyaḥ |
brahmarājanyābhyāṁ śūdrāya cāryāya ca svāya cāraṇāya ||
(*Yajurveda Vājasaneyī Saṁhitā* 26/2)

"My message for the welfare and the good of the human society is meant equally for the Brahmins, Ksatriyas, Vaisyas, Sudras, and even Panchamas, i.e. untouchables."

Many of the Vedic Sutras were revealed to many shudra and female seers. Devi Sukta, which formed the basis of Chandi, was revealed to a female seer Bak, daughter of Sage Abhrina.

Therefore, every Hindu, whoever and whatever he may be, has a right to the Vedas, and will derive his benefit, to the extent to which he can follow the Vedic ideal and practices by dint of his own merit, education and capacity.

"स्वल्पमप्यस्य धर्मस्य त्रायते महतो भयात् ।"

"Even a little of this religion saves from a great fear."

Smritis Meant to Meet the Requirements of the Epoch

The Smritis were compiled and promulgated for the good of the society, keeping in view the environment and the internal requirements suited to various ages. For this reason distinctions are to be noticed between the Smritis of the different ages. Hence the Saints have advised—

"श्रुति-स्मृति-विरोधे तु श्रुतिरेव गरीयसी ।।"

"When Srutis and Smritis differ, the injunction of the Srutis has to be accepted."

The injunctions of the Smritis, which were formulated hundreds and hundreds of years ago, for encountering the social evils of those days, are no longer sufficient to meet the requirements of the society of today. So the necessity is being felt for new Smritis, for this new era of the revival of the Hindus. If the Hindus go too slow in adopting the Vedic ideal and practices and continue to be prejudiced by the injunctions of the Smritis of good old times, then the welfare of the Hindus will assuredly be a far cry.

Caste Distinction on the Basis of Merit and Profession is Approved by the Vedas

"चातुर्वर्ण्यं मया सृष्टं गुणकर्मविभागशः ॥"

"I have ordained four castes on the basis of merit and profession", said Lord Krishna.

Why should those who were once named Shudras centuries ago because of their being uncivilized, uncultured and uneducated, be still known as such, though at present they are highly cultured, educated, endowed with higher qualities, and highly situated in different professions? On the contrary, why should not those Brahmins who have lost all virtues and professional superiority, not go down to form the fifth stratum?

Adopt Vedic Ideal

Every Hindu, advanced or backward, will have to make serious and sincere efforts to earn higher and higher virtues and cultural refinement as far as practicable, by dint of his merit, energy and enthusiasm, by strict adherence to Vedic ideals and rituals. Then and then only will the various social distinctions, originating in heredity, wealth, position, and caste be eradicated and natural unity re-gained; malice, hatred, and enmity will be stamped out; unity, friendship, and harmony will be established and, consequently, strength of cohesion and solidarity will be developed.

Religion as the Backbone of Society and Nationality

Hindu society and nationality had been organised on the basis of Truth and Religion as realised by the saints themselves. As such, religion alone is the main support of the vital energy and life of the Hindu society and nationality. The basic principle of Hindu national life is the unflinching determination to adhere to one's own religion. Hindus must firmly and determinedly stand on their spiritual and religious principles for social synthesis and nation-building purposes. In order to bring about social synthesis, discipline, national unity, and harmony, it is of foremost and pre-eminent necessity that the Hindus be united and single-minded in their religious practices.

Every Hindu must be Devoted to Divine Communion Through Prayer

Hindus whose individual, social and national life were moulded, from time immemorial, according to religious principles, with the Almighty as the central figure, have now become indifferent to and negligent in prayer and religious practice. Why shouldn't they be sinking downwards ? Which way will lead them to progress and prosperity ?

Just as the Muslims perform their Namaj (daily prayer), the Christians their prayer, similarly 'Sandhya-vandana', that is, Divine Communion through prayer, as prescribed by the Vedas, constitutes the universal and national method of Hindu prayer. The Hindus have given up 'Sandhya-vandana', due to which the very existence of the Hindus as a nation is in jeopardy. Though they are three hundred million in number, they are very weak and helpless in the face of dangers and difficulties, oppression and repression.

If the Hindus are to live, if the Hindu society is to continue to exist with its own ideal and unique characteristics, if the vast masses of the Hindu society are to be organised into a strong, powerful and undivided great nation, then every Hindu, irrespective of caste and creed, age and sex, must be devoted to prayer, both in individual and social life; everyone must be attentive, regular and steady with regard to the performance of prayer.

Vedic Prayer in the Hindu Milan Mandirs

Through the innumerable Hindu Milan Mandirs, the centres of the movement for a synthetic re-adjustment of the Hindu society, arrangements are being made to give proper training to the Hindus of all castes, both males and females, in universal, Vedic methods of Sandhya-vandana (divine communion through prayer).

Every Hindu has a right to 'Sandhya-vandana'

Every Hindu, whether a Brahmin or a Ksatrya or a Vaisya or a Shudra, whether a male or a female, has equal right to Vedic method of prayer. Every Hindu will have to take to regular prayer. Just as a man cannot maintain his physical existence without food and drink, similarly the religious and social life of the Hindus cannot exist without prayer to the Almighty according to the Vedic method. So, under the instructions and direction of Jugacharya, Hindus of every caste and creed are being given the right to Vedic prayer, and arrangements are being made to give proper training and guidance to every Hindu in this direction.

The current method of Hindu prayer is elaborate and complex. It is not possible and convenient for the Hindu masses to perform their prayer in accordance with the revealed texts. As such, this booklet is being published for the training of all Hindus, of all castes, in the simple and easy methods of performing Vedic prayer.

In this connection, the following facts are to be borne in mind—

(1) The current idea is that the females and the Shudras have got no right to the Vedas and that it is improper for them, therefore, to perform the Vedic prayer. Such an idea is absolutely baseless and unreasonable. Every Hindu has a right to the Vedas and performance of the Vedic prayer. Rather, without performing prayer, Hindus are destined to fall as they are actually doing. Right is attained through training. Hindus of all castes are being taught the methods of performing prayer through the Hindu Milan Mandirs.

(2) The current idea is that those who did not undergo the Upanayana saṁskāra or the investiture ceremony in which one is given the sacred thread, those who are not entitled to it, and those who are not initiated, have no right to the Vedic method of Divine communion through prayer. This idea is erroneous on the face of it. Every Hindu should know that there is no restriction to the Vedic method of prayer. Every Hindu, whether he is wearing the sacred thread or is not initiated, is entitled to the Vedic form of prayer. Just like 'Harinam-kirtan' (chanting of the holy name of the Supreme), the prayer to the Almighty is to be performed always and everywhere. Every Hindu, young and old, male and female, must take to the daily method of Divine communion through prayer, according to the Vedic method.

(3) Those who are given the sacred thread by their Acharyas, and thus are taught the method of Sandhya-vandana (Divine communion through prayer) are to follow that method. Those who are initiated by their Gurus will first perform the Vedic prayer, as taught by the Acharyas, and then perform the rites and repetition of the Bija-mantras, as instructed by the Guru.

Those who had undergone neither investiture with the holy thread nor initiation, will learn the following abridged method of Sandhya-vandana and strictly observe the method every dawn and nightfall.

(4) The current idea is that the Shudras and others should not pronounce. AUM. Such an idea is absolutely false. AUM is a potential sound; it is a sound identical with Brahma the Infinite or the Absolute. Just as a huge banian tree originates from a tiny seed, as small as a mustard seed, similarly all sounds originate from AUM. A—U—M=AUM. A—Brahma (the Creator); U—Vishnu (the Protector); and M—Maheshvara (the Destroyer). Meditation on and repetition of this sound is equivalent to worshipping the Almighty—the synthesis of Brahma, Vishnu and Shiva. When the word AUM is sounded, it touches all the centres from which sound arises, beginning from the umbilicus at the bottom reaching up to the edge of the lips at the top. As such, the sound AUM is considered to be the basic sound or the mother of all sounds. The Vedas originated from 'Gayatri' (the mother of the Vedas), and Gayatri originated from this sound AUM, just as the sprout comes out of the seed and the plant from the sprout. Therefore, the sound AUM is the highest denomination of the Almighty. There can be no restriction to the utterance of AUM, just as there is no restriction to the utterance of the name HARI. Hence, there is the prescription that the word AUM is to be prefixed to every Vedic mantra when pronounced for prayer purposes.

(5) The aforesaid method of 'Sandhya-vandana' may be taken recourse to both singly and jointly. Just as the Muslims and Christians, the Aryasamajists and Sikhs amongst the Hindus, perform mass-prayer, so must the mass-prayer system be introduced amongst the Hindus in general. It can be assured that through the mass-prayer system, strength of unity and solidarity will regenerate the Hindu society. Such strength existed in Hindu society, during the Vedic and subsequent periods, and that was due to a great extent to the prevalence of the mass-prayer system in those days.

(6) For the purpose just mentioned, every family must have a special room set apart for prayer, where the members of the family will have to assemble as far as practicable, and will have to perform Sandhya-vandana every morning and evening. One

of the members will have to recite the Vedic mantras and perform the Vedic rites, and the rest of the members present will have to follow him.

'आचारप्रभवो धर्मः'

The origin of Dharma is Sadachara (right conduct). Age-old redant customs, supersititions and meaningless practices, untouchability, etc., which are prevalent in society now-a-days are due to the abrogation of 'Sadachara' (right conduct). What, then, is really meant by 'Sadachara' (right conduct)? The Vedic rules and principles of right conduct as determined by the sages are conducive to self-development. Such good practices form the basis of devotional prayer and religious attainments. All religious observances of a man, if devoid of good conduct, are of no avail.

Right Conduct Constitutes an Important Element of Education and Civilization

A person of right conduct is known as gentle, civilized and cultured. Even an educated and respectable man, if he does not observe right conduct, is abused and hated in society. Highly cultured and educated people do not hesitate to mix on equal terms nor to take food and drink with those of the so-called low-caste Hindus, who are habitual the observers of Right conduct.

Sadachara or right conduct is of three kinds, viz., Physical, Mental and Verbal. They were formulated with a view to maintaining the purity of the Body, Mind and Word. Many evil and sordid practices are to be met with amongst both the high-class and the so-called backward Hindus. Those must be abandoned. This being the age of revival, re-organisation and resurrection of the Hindus, they will have to take resort to easy, simple and reasonably sound practices approved by the Vedas, giving up all complex rituals.

Hindu Welfare lies in Vedic Prayer and Practices

The all-round well-being of the Hindu society and nationality is assured if the Hindus are really and sincerely inclined towards the Vedic form of prayer and practices. Certainly they will derive the following benefits from Divine communion through prayer and practices:

1. The body will gain health and longevity.
2. The mind will be pure and steady.
3. Words uttered will be beneficial and true.
4. Their conduct will be both gentle and pleasant.
5. Idleness, luxury and inactivity will gradually vanish.
6. Daily life will be systematised and regularised.
7. Capacity to discharge duties and responsibilities will develop manifold.
8. Hindu-consciousness and affinity with the Hindu masses will grow.
9. Confidence in and devotion to Hindu sages and saints, gurus, scriptures, temples, mantras, gods, and holy-places will be generated.
10. Regard for the ancestors and a sense of pride in their glorious achievements will grow.
11. Malignity, enmity, hatred, narrow-mindedness and selfishness amongst the various sects and classes of the Hindu society will give way to mutual sympathy and friendship.
12. A sense of self-respect will be aroused and the Hindus will be encouraged to make necessary preparations for self-defence.
13. Solidarity and cohesion, both excellent ideals, will be established in Hindu Society.

धर्मोऽस्य मूलान्यसव: प्रकाण्डो वित्तानि शाखाश्छदनानि कामा: ।
यशांसि पुष्पाणि फलं च पुण्यं असौ सदाचार-तरुर्महीयान् ।।

"Right conduct may be compared with a tree of which the root is religious practices, the stem is longevity, the branches are wealth and prosperity, the flowers are reputation and fame, the leaves are peace and happiness, and the fruit is piety and righteousness." It means that it is easy for a man of right conduct to gain everything mentioned above.

The whole Life of a Hindu is Surrendered at the Feet of the Almighty

In conclusion, it may be stated that the Hindu did not keep

the Almighty and religious observances limited within a definite corner of life, so as to finish all transactions with God and perform religions observances on a fixed date and within a fixed period. Accordingly, the Hindu sages taught the Hindus that

> प्रातरुत्थाय सायाह्नं सायाह्नात् प्रातरन्ततः ।
> यत् करोमि जगन्मातस्तदेव तव पूजनम् ॥
> *prātarutthāya sāyāhnaṁ sāyāhnāt prātarantataḥ |*
> *yat karomi jaganmātastadeva tava pūjanam ||*

"Whatever we do from dawn to dusk and from dusk to dawn, everything is Thy service and worship, O Mother of the Universe."

> यत् करोषि यदश्नासि यज्जुहोषि ददासि यत् ।
> यत्तपस्यसि कौन्तेय तत्कुरुष्व मदर्पणम् ॥
> *yat karoṣi yadaśnāsi yajjuhoṣi dadāsi yat |*
> *yattapasyasi kaunteya tatkuruṣva madarpaṇam ||*

"Whatever you do, whatever you eat or drink, whatever sacrifices you perform, whatever charity you do, whatever meditation and prayer you observe, dedicate everything to the Almighty for His satisfaction."

In this way, the individual, family, and social life of the Hindus grew up, with the Almighty at the centre. Every detail of everyday life of a Hindu used to be dedicated to the Almighty in this way, and this came to be known as Hinduism.

As ill luck would have it, the Hindus have forgotten those practices, ideas and ideals at this age. They have the narrow idea now-a-days that the particular period when they devote themselves to the worship of God or to the singing of prayer-songs, they are concerned with God and religion. God and religion have nothing to do with the rest of their daily life and activities. Such a misconception must be corrected. Today, the Hindus will have to develop the all-comprehensive ideal of Hindu Dharma in and through their lives and activities. Just as one may be in communion with the Divinity through prayer, so may one be in touch with the Almighty, through the discharge of the various duties and responsibilities of life, if he dedicate each and every act to the feet of the Almighty. Therefore, just as every Hindu will have to be in communion with God through daily prayers, in the same way every activity of daily life, however trifling it may be, must be performed efficiently, honestly and sincerely, dedicating the same to the Almighty with care and deep devotion. Thus the Vedas prescribe:—

"Always be in communion with the Almighty."

If all activities are dedicated to God, the aforesaid direction of the Vedas is reflected *ipso facto* in one's life.

Hindu Daily Rites

The rites are to be performed at the time of leaving the bed. (Brahmamuhurta is one hour before sun-rise. Leave the bed before that time.)

Everyone ought to get up in the fourth quarter of the night, sit up on the bed, fully concentrate upon Gurudeva (spiritual guide) and bow down before him, reciting the following verses with full devotion:—

ओं अज्ञानतिमिरान्धस्य ज्ञानाञ्जन-शलाकया ।
चक्षुरुन्मीलितं येन तस्मै श्रीगुरवे नमः ।।

Oṁ ajñānatimirāndhasya jñānāñjana-śalākayā |
cakṣurunmīlitaṁ yena tasmai śrīgurave namaḥ ||[1]

ओं मन्त्र सत्यं पूजा सत्यं सत्यं देवो निरंजनः ।।
गुरोर्वाक्यं सदा सत्यं सत्यमेव परं पदम् ।।

Oṁ mantra satyaṁ pūjā satyaṁ satyaṁ devo niraṁjanaḥ |
gurorvākyaṁ sadā satyaṁ satyameva paraṁ padam ||[2]

ओं अखण्डमण्डलाकारं व्याप्तं येन चराचरम् ।
तत्पदं दर्शितं येन तस्मै श्रीगुरवे नमः ।।

Oṁ akhaṇḍamaṇḍalākāraṁ vyāptaṁ yena carācaram |
tatpadaṁ darśitaṁ yena tasmai śrīgurave namaḥ ||[3]

---

1. I bow down before Gurudeva who has opened my inner vision by removing the utter blindness of dark ignorance, with the help of the salve of knowledge.

2. Mantra is true, Puja is true, Brahma is true, Gurudeva's words are ever true, and the feet of the Almighty are true indeed.

3. I bow down before Gurudeva who has revealed to me the feet of the Almighty or the all-pervasive Infinite Being, who is of the form of the entire sphere.

ओं पितृ-मातृ-सुहृद्बन्धुविद्यातीर्थानि देवता ।
न तुल्यं गुरुणा शीघ्रं स्पर्शयेत्परमं पदम् ।।

Oṁ pitṛ-mātṛsuhṛdbandhuvidyātīrthāni devatā /
na tulyaṁ guruṇā śīghraṁ sparśayetparaṁ padam //[4]

ओं गुरुर्ब्रह्मा गुरुर्विष्णुः गुरुर्देवो महेश्वरः ।
गुरुरेव परं ब्रह्म तस्मै श्रीगुरवे नमः ।।

Oṁ gururbrahmā gururviṣṇuḥ gururdevo maheśvaraḥ /
gurureva paraṁ brahma tasmai śrīgurave namaḥ //[5]

ओं ध्यानमूलं गुरोर्मूर्तिः पूजामूलं गुरोः पदम् ।
मन्त्रमूलं गुरोर्वाक्यं मोक्षमूलं गुरोः कृपा ।।

Oṁ dhyānamūlaṁ gurormūrtiḥ pūjāmūlaṁ guroḥ padam /
mantramūlaṁ gurorvākyaṁ mokṣamūlaṁ guroḥ kṛpā //[6]

ओं ब्रह्मानन्दं परमसुखदं केवलं ज्ञानमूर्तिम् ।
द्वन्द्वातीतं गगनसदृशं तत्त्वमस्यादिलक्ष्यम् ।।

Oṁ brahmānandaṁ paramasukhadaṁ kevalaṁ jñānamūrtim/
dvandvātītaṁ gaganasadṛśaṁ tattvamasyādilakṣyam //[7]

ओं एकं नित्यं विमलमचलं सर्वदा साक्षिभूतम् ।
भावातीतं त्रिगुणरहितं सद्गुरुं तं नमामि ।।

Oṁ ekaṁ nityaṁ vimalamacalaṁ sarvadā sākṣibhūtam /
bhāvātītaṁ triguṇarahitaṁ sadguruṁ taṁ namāmi//[8]

---

4. Father, mother, companion, friend, learning, holy-places and the gods, cannot be compared with Gurudeva who is competent to put me in touch with the Almighty in no time.

5. I bow down before Gurudeva, who is identical with Brahma, Vishnu and Shiva and also the Supreme Brahma.

6. The form of Gurudeva forms the basis of meditation, the feet of Gurudeva form the basis of worship, the words of Gurudeva form the basis of the Mantras, and the blessings of Gurudeva form the basis of final emancipation.

7. Thou art eternal bliss, source of infinite happiness, only representation of infinite knowledge, beyond all controversies, just like the infinite horizon, and the aim of absolute knowledge.

8. I bow down before Gurudeva, who is one, eternal, purest, immovable, omnipresent, beyond all changes, and above all the three Gunas (qualities).

त्वमेव माता च पिता त्वमेव
त्वमेव बन्धुश्च सखा त्वमेव ।
त्वमेव विद्या द्रविणं त्वमेव
त्वमेव सर्वं मम देवदेव ॥

tvameva mātā ca pitā tvameva
tvameva bandhuśca sakhā tvameva |
tvameva vidyā draviṇaṁ tvameva
tvameva sarvaṁ mama devadeva. ||[9]

Later on, one should go on reciting the following verse with the thought—"I am not a gross matter, I am above birth, old age, and death, and I am the eternal, purest soul."

अहं देवो न चान्योऽस्मि ब्रह्मैवास्मि न शोकभाक् ।
सच्चिदानन्दरूपोऽस्मि नित्य-मुक्तः स्वभाववान् ॥

ahaṁ devo na cānyo'smi brahmaivāsmi na śokabhāk |
saccidānandarūpo'smi nitya-muktaḥ svabhāvavān ||

"I am none but God, I am Brahma, free from miseries; I am the Existence-Knowledge-Bliss Absolute. I am Eternal and Free."

Later on, one should pray, reciting the following verses:

ब्रह्मामुरारिस्त्रिपुरान्तकारी भानुः शशी भूमिसुतो बुधश्च ।
गुरुश्च शुक्रः शनि-राहु-केतुः कुर्वन्तु सर्वे मम सुप्रभातम् //

प्रातरुत्थाय सायाह्नं सायाह्नात् प्रातरन्ततः ।
यत्करोमि जगन्मातस्तदेव तव पूजनम् ॥

brahmāmurāristripurāntakārī bhānuḥ śaśī bhūmisuto budhaśca |
guruśca śukraḥ śani-rāhu-ketuḥ kurvantu sarve mama suprabhātam ||[10]

prātarutthāya sāyāhnaṁ sāyāhnāt prātarantataḥ |
yatkaromi jaganmātastadeva tava pūjanam ||[11]

9. Thou art my mother and father, friend and companion, learning and wealth; Thou art my all, the God of Gods.

10. "Brahma, the enemy of the demon Murari (Vishnu), and the destroyer of the demon Tripura (Shiva), the Sun, the Moon, the Mars, the Murcury, the Jupiter, the Venus, the Saturn, the Rahu and the Ketu—all of them bring forth a happy break of day."

11. "Whatever I do from dawn to dusk and from dusk to dawn, everything is Thy service and worship, O Mother of the Universe!"

Finally, the following verses are to be recited, the persons named are to be bowed down to and then the bed is to be left.

पुण्यश्लोको नलो राजा पुण्यश्लोको युधिष्ठिरः ।
पुण्यश्लोका च वैदेही पुण्यश्लोको जनार्दनः ।।
अहल्या द्रौपदी कुन्ती तारा मन्दोदरी तथा ।
पंचकन्याः स्मरेन्नित्यं महापातकनाशनम् ।।

puṇyaśloko nalo rājā puṇyaśloko yudhiṣṭhiraḥ |
puṇyaślokā ca vaidehī puṇyaśloko janārdanaḥ ||[12]
ahalyā draupadī kuntī tārā mandodarī tathā |
paṁcakanyāḥ smarennityaṁ mahāpātakanāśanam ||[13]

Purification by Ablution

Everyone should bathe after answering the call of nature and cleansing his teeth. He who is unable to bathe because of illness or any other inconvenience, should put off the clothes worn at night and wear clothes cleanly washed. One should pray as follows while bathing:

ओं गंगे च यमुने चैव गोदावरि सरस्वति ।
नर्मदे सिन्धु कावेरि जलेऽस्मिन् सन्निधिं कुरु ।।

Oṁ gaṁge ca yamune caiva godāvari sarasvati |
narmade sindhu kāveri jale'smin sannidhiṁ kuru ||[14]

ओं कुरुक्षेत्र-गया-गंगा-प्रभास-पुष्कराणि च ।
तीर्थान्येतानि पुण्यानि स्नानकाले भवन्त्विह ।।

Oṁ kurukṣetra-gayā-gaṁgā-prabhāsa-puṣkarāṇi ca |
tīrthānyetāni puṇyāni snānakāle bhavantvih ||[15]

---

12. "I bow down to King Nala, Yudhishthira, and Lord Krishna of sacred celebrity."

13. "I respectfully remember the five names of the sacred daughters, viz., Ahalya, Draupadi, Kunti, Tara, and Mandodari, whereby the greatest sin is destroyed."

14. "The Ganga, the Jamuna, the Godavari, the Sarasvati, the Narmada, the Sindhu, and the Kaveri (all being the names of holy Indian rivers along whose courses the ancient Aryan culture developed)—I invoke all of you in this water."

15. "Let Kurukshetra, Gaya, Ganga, Prabhasa and Pushkara—all these holy places be present here at the time of bathing."

THE DAILY PROCEDURE FOR VEDIC "SANDHYA-VANDANA"

(Divine Communion Through Prayer)

After bath, dry, pure, and clean clothes are to be worn. If indoors, then taking water in water-vessels, usually used in making offerings, and sitting in a seat made of either kusha grass or on a carpet or deer-skin one should perform one's 'Sandhya-vandana'; if out of doors, on a journey or in some foreign place, then sitting close to some river or tank, one should be in Divine communion through prayer. If no water is available for bathing and rinsing purposes, then even without water, one should be in Divine communion through prayer just at the appointed hour everyday. Three hours in the morning (i.e., beginning from one hour before the sunrise, up to two hours after the sunrise) and two hours in the evening (i.e., beginning from one hour before the sunset, up to one hour after the sunset) have been prescribed as the time for Sandhya-vandana. Prayer must have to be offered within the specified periods every dawn and dusk. He who is practised may perform the rite, standing in navel-deep water, after bath. Brahmins, Ksatriyas, Vaishyas and Shudras, male and female alike, are equally entitled to perform Sandhya-vandana or Divine prayer everyday, failing which the transgressor's offence will amount to an act of sin and crime.

Prayer is to Begin with Achamana

Achmana is performed by taking a sip of water with the right palm and then rinsing the mouth with it. This is to be done three times, after reciting each one of the following three Mantras, one after another:

ओं अमृतोपस्तरणमसि स्वाहा ।
ओं अमृतापिधानमसि स्वाहा ।
ओं सत्यं यशः श्रीः मयि श्रयतां स्वाहा ।

Oṁ amṛtopastaraṇamasi svāhā |
Oṁ amṛtāpidhānamasi svāhā |

Oṁ satyaṁ yaśaḥ śrīḥ mayi śrayatāṁ svāhā/[1]
(*Gṛhya Sūtra*)

Next process is Pranayama (Practising Control of the Vital Energy by Regulating Breath)

One is to sit erect (keeping the neck, chest and head in the same straight line) on one's seat, with his eyes shut and mouth closed, then to go on exhaling and simultaneously repeating the Mantra AUM. He should then stop the breath and go on repeating the Mantra Aum, and, finally, keep inhaling again while repeating the Mantra Aum at the same time. The Mantra AUM is to be repeated four times at the time of inhaling air, eight times during the time when the breath is stopped, and sixteen times at the time of exhaling again. In this way Pranayama (i.e., the complete process of exhaling, stopping, and inhaling air) has to be repeated three times continuously, in every sitting. Performance of Pranayama makes the body and mind calm, relaxed and strong.

Next process is Punarachamana (Repetition of Achamana)

Repetition of rinsing the mouth has to be performed once again by reciting the following Mantra:

ओं शन्नो देवीरभिष्टय आपो भवन्तु पीतये
शं योरभि स्रवन्तु नः ।

Oṁ śanno devīrabhiṣṭaya āpo bhavantu pītaye
śaṁ yorabhi sravantu naḥ /[2]

Next process is Indriyasparsha (i.e., Introverting the Tendencies of the Sense-organs by Touching the Body)

The fingers of the right palm are to be wetted and with the wet fingres, the following parts of the body are to be touched serially: viz., mouth, nose, eyes, ears, navel, chest, neck, head,

1. "O Almighty! Thou art the protector and rearer of living beings. Be gracious unto me and endow me with truth, fame, beauty and prosperity."

2. "Let the all-pervading and all-manifesting Almighty be beneficent and ever-blessed unto us, and grant us the objects and also the happiness we pray for.

arms, palm and back of the palms. Simultaneously and one after another the following Mantras are to be recited:

ओं वाक् वाक् । ओं प्राणः प्राणः । ओं चक्षुः चक्षुः ।
ओं श्रोत्रम् श्रोत्रम् । ओं नाभिः । ओं हृदयम् ।
ओं कण्ठः । ओं शिरः । ओं बाहुभ्यां यशोबलम् ।
ओं करतल-करपृष्ठे ।

Oṁ vāk vāk| Oṁ prāṇaḥ prāṇaḥ| Oṁ cakṣuḥ cakṣuḥ|
Oṁ śrotram śrotram| Oṁ nābhiḥ| Oṁ hṛdayam|
Oṁ kaṇṭhaḥ| Oṁ śiraḥ| Oṁ bāhubhyāṁ yaśobalam|
Oṁ karatala-karapṛṣṭhe|[3]

Next Process is Marjana (i.e., Cleansing)

The fingers are to be dipped in water which is to be sprinkled by the fingers over the head, eyes, chest, navel, legs, and again over the head, by reciting the following Mantras. If the mind be concentrated on the different parts of the body, while the Mantras are being uttered, then the strength of determination—unshakeable resolution—is acquired.

ओं भूः पुनातु शिरसि । ओं भुवः पुनातु नेत्रयोः ।
ओं स्वः पुनातु कण्ठे । ओं महः पुनातु हृदये ।
ओं जनः पुनातु नाभ्याम् । ओं तपः पुनातु पादयोः ।
ओं सत्यं पुनातु पुनः शिरसि । ओं खं ब्रह्म पुनातु ब्रह्म सर्वत्र ।

Oṁ bhūḥ punātu śirasi| Oṁ bhuvaḥ punātu netrayoḥ|
Oṁ svaḥ punātu kaṇṭhe| Oṁ mahaḥ punātu hṛdaye|
Oṁ janaḥ punātu nābhyām| Oṁ tapaḥ punātu pādayoḥ|
Oṁ satyaṁ punātu punaḥ śirasi| Oṁ khaṁ brahma punātu brahma sarvatra|[4]

Then the following Mantras are to be recited:

ओं भूः । ओं भुवः । ओं स्वः । ओं महः । ओं जनः ।
ओं तपः । ओं सत्यम् ।

3. "O Almighty! Strengthen my words, life, eyes, ears, neck, heart, throat and head. Bestow renown and strength on my arms; I shall perform religious rites by the palm and back of the palm."

4. "O Almighty! Purify and strengthen my head, eyes, throat, chest, navel, legs, and all limbs beginning with the head."

Oṁ bhūḥ/ Oṁ bhuvaḥ/ Oṁ svaḥ/ Oṁ mahaḥ/ Oṁ janaḥ/
Oṁ tapaḥ/ Oṁ satyam/[5]

Next Trocess is Aghamarshsna (i.e. Expiation)

Sin is to be expiated by repeating the following Mantras, simultaneously concentrating upon the truth of the Universe.

ओ ऋतं च सत्यं चाभीद्धात् तपसोऽध्यजायत ततो
रात्र्यजायत ततः समुद्रोऽर्णवः ।।
ओं समुद्राद् अर्णवाद्अधि संवत्सरो अजायत अहोरात्राणि
विदधद्विश्वस्य मिषतो वशी ।। ओं सूर्याचन्द्रमसौ धाता
यथापूर्वमकल्पयत् दिवं च पृथिवीं च अन्तरिक्षमथो स्वः ।।

Oṁ ṛtaṁ ca satyaṁ cābhīddhāt, tapaso'dhyajāyata
tato rātryajāyata tataḥ samudro'rṇavaḥ//
Oṁ samudrād arṇavādadhi saṁvatsaro ajāyata
ahorātrāṇi vidadhadviśvasya miṣato vaśī//
Oṁ sūryācandramasau dhātā yathāpūrvamakalpayat
divaṁ ca pṛthivīṁ ca antarikṣamatho svaḥ//[6]

Next Process is Suryyopasthan

One is to continue concentrating upon the desired Divine form placed at the centre of the Solar Sphere and to go on reciting the following Mantra:

ओं उदु त्य जातवेदसं देवं वहन्ति केतवः दृशे विश्वाय सूर्यम् ।
ओं उद्वयं तमसस्परि ज्योतिष्पश्यन्त उत्तरम् देवं देवत्रा
सूर्यमगन्म ज्योतिरुत्तमम् ।। ओं चित्रं देवानामुदगादनीकं
चक्षुर्मित्रस्य वरुणस्याग्नेः । आप्रा द्यावापृथिवी अन्तरिक्षं
सूर्य आत्मा जगतस्तस्थुषश्च स्वाहा ।।

5. "The Almighty represents life, purity, and bliss, He is the most Supreme, universal father, omniscient, and eternal."

6. The Absolute manifested Himself as the Phenomena through His natural tendency for multiplication and enjoyment. Then followed darkness and subtle water-consciousness which were followed by the origin of time-consciousness manifested as diurnal and nocturnal movement. The Almighty has created the Sun, the Moon, the heavens, the world, the horizon, and the other worlds, just as He created these in the first Kalpa (cycle of existence)."

Oṁ udu tyaṁ jātavedasaṁ devaṁ vahanti ketavaḥ dṛśe viśvāya sūryam/ Oṁ udvayaṁ tamasaspari jyotiṣpaśyanta uttaram devaṁ devatrā sūryamaganma jyotiruttamam/ Oṁ citraṁ devānāmudagādanīkaṁ cakṣurmitrasya varuṇasyāgneḥ/ āprā dyāvāprithivī antarikṣaṁ sūrya ātmā jagatastasthuṣaśca svāhā/[7]

Then, one should pray and recite the following Mantra:

ओं तच्चक्षुर्देवहितं पुरस्ताच्छुक्रमुच्चरत् ।
पश्येम शरदः शतं जीवेम शरदः शतम् ।
श्रृणुयाम शरदः शतं प्रब्रवाम शरदः शतम्
अदीनाः स्याम शरदः शतं भूयश्च शरदः शतात् ।।

Oṁ taccakṣurdevahitaṁ, purastācchūkramuccarat/ paśyema śaradaḥ śataṁ, jīvema śaradaḥ śatam/ śṛṇuyāma śaradaḥ śataṁ, prabravāma śaradaḥ śatam adīnāḥ syāma śaradaḥ śataṁ, bhūyaśca śaradaḥ śatāt//[8]

Later on, one should bow down and go on reciting the following:

ओं ब्रह्मणे नमः । ओं आचार्येभ्यो नमः । ओं ऋषिभ्यो नमः ।
ओं देवेभ्यो नमः । ओं वेदेभ्यो नमः ।

Oṁ brahmaṇe namaḥ/ Oṁ ācāryebhyo namaḥ/ Oṁ ṛṣibhyo namaḥ/ Oṁ devebhyo namaḥ/ Oṁ vedebhyo namaḥ/[9]

Next Process is Gayatri Japa (i.e., Repetition of Gayatri)

The lumionous form of the Gurudeva (spiritual guide) or

---

7. "O God! Thou whose luminous representation the Sun is and whose glory the universe proclaims, Thou art Knowledge-Bliss-Absolute, beyond the region of darkness; Thine supreme luminosity illumines the soul of the wise and the virtuous. Thou art a surprise to the high and to those well-versed in the Vedas. Thou art the vision of the Sun, the Neptune (Sea-God) and the Fire-God; Thou art the sustainer of the heavens, the earth and of the middle region; Thou art the soul of the movable and the immovable, let us reach Thee."

8. "O Omniscient Lord! Let us witness your glory for hundred autumns; let us live hundred autumns let us sing your glory for hundred autumns, let us live ever more than hundred autumns in this way."

9. "I bow down to the Brahma, the Acharyas, the Rishis, the Gods, and the Vedas."

that of one's desired deity placed at the centre of the Solar sphere, is to be thought of in the heart of hearts, and the following Gayatri Mantra is to be recited at least ten times.

ओं भूर्भुवः स्वः तत्सवितुर्वरेण्यं भर्गो देवस्य धीमहि धियो यो नः
प्रचोदयात् ।।

Oṁ bhūrbhuvaḥ svaḥ, tatsaviturvareṇyaṁ bhargo devasya dhīmahi dhiyo yo naḥ pracodayāt//[10]

Then, Divine communion through prayer, is to be concluded, by bowing down to the Almighty and reciting the following Mantras:

ओं नमः शम्भवाय च मयोभवाय च नमः शंकराय च
मयस्कराय च नमः शिवाय च शिवतराय च ।।

Oṁ namaḥ śambhavāya ca mayobhavāya ca namaḥ
śaṅkarāya ca mayaskarāya ca namaḥ śivāya ca
śivatarāya ca//[11]

Concluding Rite

One should express universal love and fellow-feeling by making the following proposals with the greatest delight:

सर्वेषां मंगलं भूयात् सर्वे सन्तु निरामयाः ।
सर्वे भद्राणि पश्यन्तु मा कश्चित् दुःखभाग् भवेत् ।।

sarveṣāṁ maṅgalaṁ bhūyāt sarve santu nirāmayāḥ /
sarve bhadrāṇi paśyantu mā kaścit duḥkhabhāg bhavet //[1]

नन्दन्तु सर्वभूतानि निरातंकानि सन्तु च ।
प्रीतिरस्तु परस्परं सिद्धिरस्तु च कर्मणाम् ।।

nandantu sarvabhūtāni nirātaṅkāni santu ca /
prītirastu parasparaṁ siddhirastu ca karmaṇām //[2]

---

10. "He, who is the creator of the three worlds, and gives impetus to our intuition, may I be in communion with His supreme luminosity.

11. "I bow down to the Almighty—who represents eternal bliss, happiness and peace; and who is all good and immensely propitious."

1. Let everybody be blessed, let everybody be free from disease, let there be prosperity everywhere, let nobody suffer.

2. "Let everybody be happy and free from anxiety, let there be mutual fellow-feeling and let everybody be successful in his mission."

स्वस्त्यस्तु राज्ञो नित्यशः शं प्रजाभ्यस्तथेवास्तु ।
स्वस्त्यस्तु द्विपदे नित्यं शान्तिरस्तु चतुष्पदे ।।

svastyastu rājño nityaśaḥ śam prajābhyastathevāstu |
svastyastu dvipade nityaṁ śāntirastu catuṣpade ||[3]

शान्तिरस्तु नो देवस्य भूर्भुवः स्वः शिवं तथा ।
सर्वतः शान्तिरस्तु नः सौम्या भवन्तु भूतानि ।।

śāntirastu no devasya bhūrbhuvaḥ svaḥ śivaṁ tathā |
sarvataḥ śāntirastu naḥ saumyā bhavantu bhūtāni ||[4]

त्वं देवो जगतः स्रष्टा पाता दैवत्वमेवहि ।
प्रजाः पालय देवेश शान्ति कुरु जगत्पते ।।

tvaṁ devo jagataḥ sraṣṭā pātā daivatvamevahi |
prajāḥ pālaya deveśa śāntiṁ kuru jagatpate ||[5]

यो मे अद्य स्निह्यते तस्य शिवमस्तु सदा भुवि ।
यश्च मां द्वेष्टि लोकेऽस्मिन् सोऽपि भद्राणि पश्यतु ।।
ओं शान्तिः शान्तिः शान्तिः हरिः ओं ।

yo me adya snihyate tasya śivamastu sadā bhuvi |
yaśca māṁ dveṣṭi loke'smin so'pi bhadrāṇi paśyatu ||[6]
Oṁ śāntiḥ, śāntiḥ, śāntiḥ, Hari Oṁ |

Oṁ vīrayamasi vīryaṁ mayi dhehi
Oṁ balamasi balaṁ mayi dhehi
Oṁ tejo'si tejo mayi dhehi
Oṁ ojo'si ojo mayi dhehi
Oṁ manyurasi manyuṁ mayi dhehi
Oṁ saho'asi saho mayi dhehi.[7]

---

3. "Let the Kings who protect their subjects prosper everyday and the people be in peace. Let the bipeds prosper daily and the quadrupeds be peaceful."

4. "Let our gods be in peace, let the three spheres be peaceful, let ourselves have peace everywhere, and let the living beings be serene.

5. "Lord! Thou art the creator and protector of the world, Thou art the sustainer and godliness, itself, Thou the God of gods, protect the people and bring about peace in the world."

6. "Let him always be peaceful on the earth, one who is friendly unto me today; let him also be peaceful who is hostile to me in the world.

7. O Lord, Thou art the embodiment of energy, strength, glory, resolute anger and patience. May we be ever blessed with those virtues.

VEDIC HAVANA

Hindus of all castes and creeds will assemble at a well-arranged common meeting-place, on special or auspicious festive days, and jointly perform the following Yajna (sacrifice) with material offerings. The sacrificer will have to pronounce the Mantras aloud and the Hindu assembly will have to repeat those Mantras in chorus and throw the offerings in the sacrificial fire simultaneously, praying for progress and resurrection, fortune and success, unity and friendship, and strength and peace of the entire Hindu nationality.

The Yajna is to begin with the Following Prayer for Peace

ओं सह नाववतु सह नौ भुनक्तु सह वीर्यं करवावहै ।
तेजस्विनावधीतमस्तु मा विद्विषावहै ।।
ओं पूर्णमदः पूर्णमिदं पूर्णात् पूर्णमुदच्यते ।
पूर्णस्य पूर्णमादाय पूर्णमेवावशिष्यते ।।
ओं शान्तिः शान्तिः शान्तिः हरिः ओम्

Oṁ saha nāvavatu saha nau bhunaktu saha vīryaṁ karavāvahai|
tejasvināvadhītamastu mā vidviṣāvahai ||
Oṁ pūrṇamadaḥ pūrṇamidaṁ pūrṇāt pūrṇamudacyate |
pūrṇasya pūrṇamādāya pūrṇamevāvaśiṣyate||
Oṁ śāntiḥ śāntiḥ śāntiḥ hariḥ oṁ.[1]

The Next Process is Achamana

As usual Achamana or rinsing the mouth has to be performed by reciting each one of the following Mantras once only.

ओं अमृतोपस्तरणमसि स्वाहा ।
ओं अमृतापिधानमसि स्वाहा ।
ओं सत्यं यशः श्रीर्मयि श्रयतां स्वाहा ।

Oṁ amritopastaraṇamasi svāhā|
Oṁ amritāpidhānamasi svāhā|
Oṁ satyaṁ yaśaḥ śrīrmayi śrayatāṁ svāhā|

---

1. "Save us jointly, rear us jointly, unite and strengthen us. Let us not end one another. Peace! Peace! Peace!"

Next Process is Indriyasparsha

The following parts of the body viz., the mouth, nose, eyes, ears, arms, knees, and the whole body, are to be serially touched with wet fingers and the following mantras are to be recited:

ओं वाङ्मे आस्येऽस्तु। ओं नसोर्मे प्राणोऽस्तु। ओं अक्ष्णोर्मे चक्षुरस्तु।
ओं कर्णयोर्मे श्रोत्रमस्तु। ओं बाह्वोर्मे बलमस्तु। ओं उर्वोर्मे ओजोऽस्तु।

Oṁ vāṅme āsye'stu/ *Oṁ nasorme prāṇo'stu/*
Oṁ akṣṇorme cakṣurastu/ *Oṁ karṇayorme śrotramastu/*
Oṁ bāhvorme balamastu/ *Oṁ urvorme ojo'stu/*[2]

ओं अरिष्टानि मेऽङ्गानि तनुस्तन्वा मे सह सन्तु।

Oṁ ariṣṭāni me'aṅgāni tanustanvā me saha santu/[3]

Next Process is Igniting Fire

The pieces of wood meant for sacrificial fire and piled upon the sacrificial altar are to be ignited by the flame of burning camphor with the recitation of the following mantras:

ओं भूर्भुवः स्वः
ओं भूर्भुवः स्वः द्यौरिव भूम्ना पृथिवीव वरिम्ना
तस्यास्ते पृथिवी देवयजनि पृष्ठेऽग्निमन्नादमन्नादयादधे/

Oṁ bhūrbhuvaḥ svaḥ
Oṁ bhūrbhuvaḥ svaḥ dyauriva bhūmnā prithivīva varimnā
tasyāste prithivī devayajani priṣṭhe'gnimannādamannādayā-dadhe/[4] *Yajurveda*-3/5

---

2. The one undivided pervades the entire universe and interpenetrates the atoms. Infinity comes out of Infinity. Infinity minus Infinity leaves Infinity.

"Let my tougue continue to possess the capacity to sing your glory."

"Let my sense of smell continue to have its capacity to inhale the cosmic energy."

"Let my eyes be capable of Divine vision."

"Let my ears continue to be capable of receiving the cosmic sound."

3. "Let my arms have strength."

"Let my thighs continue to be strong."

"Let the vital energy of all my limbs be intact."

4. "The worlds are as spacious as the horizon, those three are to be regarded as the mother earth herself. The sacrificial altar over the surface of the mother earth is the place where I ignite the fire."

Next Process is Vyajana (i.e., Fanning)

Fire is to be kept burning and fuelled by offering small pieces of wood and small quantities of camphor and reciting the following mantras in the process:

ओं उद्बुध्यस्वाग्ने प्रतिजागृहि त्वमिष्टापूर्ते संसृजेथामयं च ।

Oṁ udbudhyasvāgne pratijāgṛhi tvamiṣṭāpūrte saṁsṛjethāmayaṁ ca/

अस्मिन् सधस्थे अध्युत्तरस्मिन् विश्वेदेवा यजमानश्च सीदत ।।

asmin sadhasthe adhyuttarasmin viśvedevā yajamānaśca sīdata//[5]

Yajurveda-15/54

Next process is Samidahuti (i.e., Offering Pieces of Wood Specially meant for Sacrifice)

Three pieces of wood, each having the length equal to the breadth of eight fingers of the palm, are to be dipped in clarified butter and offered to the fire (each at a time).

The following mantra is to be recited at the time of offering the first piece of wood:

ओं अयन्त इध्म आत्मा जातवेदस्तेनेध्यस्व वर्द्धस्व चेद्ध वर्द्धय चास्मान् प्रजया पशुभिर्ब्रह्मवर्चसेनान्नाद्येन समेधय स्वाहा । इदमग्नये जातवेदसे । इदन्न मम ।

Oṁ ayanta idhma ātmā jātavedastenedhyasva vardhasva ceddha varddhaya cāsmān prajayā paśubhirbrahmavarcasenānnādmena samedhaya svāhā/ idamagnaye jātavedase/ idanna mama/[6]

The second piece of wood is to be offered by reciting the following mantras:

ओं समिधाग्निं दुवस्यत घृतैर्बोधयतातिथिम् ।
अस्मिन् हव्या जुहोतन स्वाहा, इदमग्नये जातवेदसे इदन्न मम ।।

5. "O Fire! Blaze up and arise: Thou art the inner principle of all constructive works and receptacle of sacrificial offerings. Let all gods and sacrificers take their seats in the northern side of this assembly."

6. "O Fire! This piece of wood is your support—flare up and rise with this and develop us, multiply our progeny and cattle, develop our knowledge of Divinity, increase our food-staff, and thus help us progress in every way. It is not mine, it belongs to you."

ओं सुसमिद्धाय शोचिषे घृतं तीव्रं जुहोतन अग्नये जातवेदसे स्वाहा ।
इदमग्नये जातवेदसे इदन्न मम ॥

Oṁ samidhāgniṁ duvasyata ghṛtairbodhayatātithim /
asmin havyā juhotana svāhā, idamagnaye jātavedase idanna mama//
Oṁ susamiddhāya śociṣe ghṛtaṁ tīvraṁ juhotana agnaye jātavedase svāhā / idamagnaye jātavedase idanna mama //[7]

The third piece of wood is to be offered by reciting the following mantras:

ओं तन्त्वा समिद्भिरङ्गिरो घृतेन वर्द्धयामसि । बृहच्छोचायविष्ठ्य स्वाहा । इदमग्नयेऽङ्गिरसे इदन्न मम ॥

Oṁ tantvā samidbhiraṅgiro ghṛtena varddhayāmasi/ bṛhaccho-cāyaviṣṭhya svāhā / idamagnaye'ṅgirase idanna mama //[8]

Next Process is Ghreetahuti (*i.e., Offering Clarified Butter*)

The following mantras are to be recited and clarified butter is to be offered five times:

ओं अयन्त इध्म आत्मा जातवेदस्तेनेध्यस्व वर्द्धस्व चेद्ध वर्द्धय चास्मान् प्रजया पशुभिर्ब्रह्मवर्चसे नान्नाद्येन समेधय स्वाहा—इदमग्नये जातवेदसे इदन्न मम ।

Oṁ ayanta idhma ātmā jātavedastenedhyasva varddhasva ceddha varddhaya cāsmān prajayā paśubhirbrahmavarcase nānnādyena samedhaya svāhā—idamagnaye jātavedase idanna mama/

Next process is Jalasinchana (*i.e., Sprinkling Water*)

Water is to be sprinkled in different directions of the sacrificial pit by reciting the following mantras in due order:

---

7. "O Fire arising out of the burning pieces of wood! Thou, our guest, be satiated by the offering of clarified butter. I have been offering it to you. It belongs to you and not to me."

8. "O Messanger! We have been arousing you by sacrificial wood and clarified butter. Thou art mighty and luminous, we have been making sacrificial offering to you. This belongs to you the messanger, and not to me."

(Greetahuti mantra is the same as that of offering the first piece of wood.)

ओं अदितेऽनुमन्यस्व । ओं अनुमतेऽनुमन्यस्व / ओं सरस्वत्यनुमन्यस्व ।
ओं देवः सवितः प्रसुव यज्ञं प्रसुव यज्ञपतिं भगाय । दिव्यो गन्धर्वः केतपुः
केतं नः पुनातु वाचस्पतिर्वाचं नः स्वदतु ।

Oṁ adite'numanyasva /
Oṁ anumate'numanyasva /
Oṁ sarasvatyanumanyasva /
Oṁ devaḥ savitaḥ prasuva yajñaṁ prasuva yajñapatiṁ bhagāya / divyo gandharvaḥ ketapuḥ ketaṁ naḥ punātu vācaspatirvācaṁ naḥ svadatu /[9]

ओं अग्नये स्वाहा । इदमग्नये इदन्न मम ।
ओं सोमाय स्वाहा । इदम् सोमाय इदन्न मम ।
ओं प्रजापतये स्वाहा । इदं प्रजापतये इदन्न मम ।
ओं इन्द्राय स्वाहा । इदं इन्द्राय इदन्न मम ।

Oṁ agnaye svāhā/ idamagnaye idanna mama/
Oṁ somāya svāhā/ idaṁ somāya idanna mama/
Oṁ prajāpataye svāhā/ idaṁ prajāpataye idanna mama/
Oṁ indrāya svāhā/ idam indrāya idanna mama/[10]

Next process is Byariti ahuti (i.e., recitation of three fundamental symbolic sounds at the time of performing sacrifices)

The following mantras are to be recited:

ओं सूर्यो ज्योतिर्ज्योतिः सूर्यः स्वाहा ।
ओं सूर्यो वर्चो ज्योतिर्वर्चः स्वाहा ।
ओं ज्योतिः सूर्यः सूर्यो ज्योतिः स्वाहा ।

Oṁ sūryyo jyotirjyotiḥ sūryyaḥ svāhā /
Oṁ sūryyo varco jyotirvarcaḥ svāhā /
Oṁ jyotiḥ sūryyaḥ sūryyo joytiḥ svāhā /

---

9. "O Mother of Gods! Thou conceive. O Conception! Be conceived. O Sarasvati (Goddess of Learning)! Conceive. O Divine Sun! Grace the Yajna and the performer of Yajna for the sake of prosperity. Let the residents of heaven glorify us and the God of speech regulate and sanctify our tongue.

10. "Offerings to Agni (Fire). It belongs to Agni and not to me. Offerings to the Moon. It belongs to the Moon and not to me. Offerings to Prajapati (Lord of progeny)—It belongs to Prajapati and not to me. Offerings to Indra (the King of the gods). It belongs to Indra not to me.

ओं सजुर्देवेन सवित्रा सजुरुषसेन्द्रवत्या जुषाणः सूर्यं वेतु स्वाहा ।

Oṁ sajurdevena savitrā sajuruṣasendravatyā juṣāṇaḥ sūrya vetu svāhā/[11]

Next, the following mantras are to be recited:

ओं अग्निर्ज्योतिः ज्योतिरग्निः स्वाहा ।
ओं अग्निर्वर्चो ज्योतिर्वर्चः स्वाहा ।
ओं ज्योतिरग्निः अग्निर्ज्योतिः स्वाहा ।
ओं सजुर्देवेन सवित्रा सजुः रात्रेन्द्रवत्या जुषाणो अग्निर्वेतु स्वाहा ।

Oṁ agnirjyotiḥ jyotiragniḥ svāhā /
Oṁ agnirvarco jyotirvarcaḥ svāhā /
Oṁ jyotiragniḥ agnirjyotiḥ svāhā /
Oṁ sajurdevena savitrā sajuḥ rātrendravatyā juṣāṇo agnirvetu svāhā/[12]

Then the following mantras are to be recited and offerings are to be thrown into the fire:

ओं भूरग्नये प्राणाय स्वाहा । इदमग्नये प्राणाय इदन्न मम ।
ओं भुवर्वायवेऽपानाय स्वाहा । इदं वायवे अपानाय इदन्न मम ।

Oṁ bhūragnaye prāṇāya svāhā/
idamagnaye prāṇāya idanna mama/
Oṁ bhuvarvāyave'pānāya svāhā / idaṁ vāyave apānāya idanna mama/

ओं स्वरादित्याय व्यानाय स्वाहा । इदं आदित्याय व्यानाय इदन्न मम ।

Oṁ svarādityāya vyānāya svāhā/
idaṁ ādityāya vyānāya idanna mama/

ओं भूर्भुवः स्वरग्निर्वाय्वादित्येभ्यः प्राणापानव्यानेभ्यः स्वाहा ।
इदमग्निवायवादित्येभ्य इदन्न मम ।

Oṁ bhū:-bhuvaḥ svaragnirvayavādityebhyaḥ prāṇāpānavyānebhyaḥ svāhā/ idamagnivāyavādityebhyaḥ idanna mama/[13]

---

11. "We are offering these sacrificial articles with a view to obeying the orders of the all-pervading Supreme Soul, who is identical with the Sun and his lustre; by doing this we shall be blessed and be rid of illness."

12. "We are making these burnt-offerings with a view to obeying the orders of the Supreme who is like Fire; by doing this we shall be blessed.

"Offerings to Agni, which is the inner principle of the earth. These belong to the soul of Agni and not to me."

13. "Offerings to the atmospheric energy, which is working as the

Next, the following mantras are to be recited while pouring oblations on the fire:

ओं आपोज्योती रसोऽमृतं ब्रह्मभूर्भुवः स्वरोम् स्वाहा ।

Oṁ āpojyotī raso'mṛtaṁ brahmabhūrbhuvaḥ svarom svāhā/[14]

Next Process is Gayatri Ahuti (Reciting the Gayatri)

The Gayatri, which runs as follows, is to be recited three times:

ओं भूर्भुवः स्वः तत्सवितुर्वरेण्यं भर्गो देवस्य धीमहि । धियो यो नः प्रचोदयात् ।

Oṁ bhūrbhuvaḥ svaḥ tatsaviturvareṇyaṁ bhargo devasya dhīmahi dhiyo yo naḥ pracodayāt/

Next process is Purnahuti (i.e., Full or Final Offering)

This offering is to be made three times, by reciting the following mantras every time:

ओं सर्वं वै पूर्णं स्वाहा ।

Oṁ sarvaṁ vai pūrṇaṁ svāhā/[15]
(Give ahuti after reading this mantra 3 times)

Next process is Ghrita Mrakshana
(i.e., Smearing the Body with Clarified Butter)

Clarified butter thrown earlier in water during the performance has to be taken by both the palms, the palms are to be rubbed against each other and slightly heated in fire, and then with such palms, hands, feet and other limbs are to be

---

excretory energy of the body. These belong to that energy and not to me."

"Offerings to the Solar energy, working as the vital energy of the body. These belong to that energy and not to me."

"Offerings to all the three forms of energy corresponding to the three regions. These belong to Agni, Vayu (atmosphere) and the Sun and not to me.

14. "Almighty is the repository of everything; He is the immanent and eternal Bliss. This offering is meant for the beneficial influence of Fire, Air, and Sun, and also for the sound working of the vital energy, excretory energy and the energy diffused all over the body."

For the meaning of Gayatri, see page 22.

15. "Let everything be definitely fulfilled."

rubbed, reciting the following seven mantras. In this manner clarified butter is to be smeared all over the body.

ओं तनुपा अग्नेऽसि तन्वं मे पाहि।
ओं आयुर्दा अग्नेऽस्यायुर्मे देहि।
ओं वर्चोदाग्नेऽसि वर्चो मे देहि।
ओं अग्ने यन्मे तन्वाह उनं तन्म आपृण।

Oṁ tanupā agne asi tanvaṁ me pāhi/
Oṁ ayurdā agne asyāyurme dehi/
Oṁ varcodāgne'si varcome dehi/
Oṁ agne yanme tanvāha unaṁ tanma āpṛṇa/

ओं मेधां मे देवः सविता आदधातु। ओं मेधान्मे देवी सरस्वती आदधातु। ओं मेधां मे अश्विनौ देवावाधत्तां पुस्करस्रजौ।

Oṁ medhāṁ me devaḥ savitā ādadhātu/
Oṁ medhān me devī sarasvatī ādadhātu/
Oṁ medhāṁ me aśvinau devāvāvadhattāṁ puskarasrajau/[16]

Next, the Following Mantras are to be Recited

ओं ब्रह्मार्पणं ब्रह्महविर्ब्रह्माग्नौ ब्रह्मणाहुतम्।
ब्रह्मैव तेन गन्तव्यं ब्रह्मकर्म समाधिना।
ओं तत्सत् हरिः ओं

Oṁ brahmārpaṇaṁ brahmahavirbrahmāgnau brahmaṇāhutam /
brahmaiva tena gantavyaṁ brahmakarma samādhinā /
Oṁ tat sat hariḥ Oṁ /[17]

Finally, the peace prayer is to be recited, as mentioned earlier on page 23.

---

16. "O body-preserving Fire! Protect my body. O life-prolonging Fire! Grant me longevity. O energizing Fire! Grant me energy! O Fire! Supplement everything and thereby completely remove every drawback. Let the Sun God grant me acumen. Let the Goddess of Learning Sarasvati grant me genius. Let the lotus-garlanded two sons of Aswini (the Divine Healers) grant me comprehension."

17. "Thou art Brahma, to whom all offerings are made; clarified butter is Brahma; fire is Brahma; and the sacrificer to Brahma. The person who in all his activities is solely devoted to Brahma, merges into Brahma."

PANCHA-YAJNA VIDHI

(METHODS OF FIVE KINDS OF SACRIFICES)

The Hindu sages have classified the various duties and responsibilities of a Hindu life into five groups and have denominated them Pancha-Yajna (five kinds of daily duties). The injunction of the Hindu scriptures is that a man is born with five kinds of debts, viz., debt to divinity, debt to sages, debt to ancestors, debt to the people, and debt to the other living beings. Men become entitled to liberation by gradual paying off of these five kinds of debts by observing the five kinds of yajnas or sacrifices. It is imperative on the part of every Hindu to perform Pancha-Yajna as far as practicable in everyday life.

Brahma-Yajna

To be in Divine Communion through prayer (daily, regularly and punctually) is known as Brahma-Yajna. By the performance of this Yajna the debt to Divinity is paid off. Brahma-Yajna is completed by being in Divine communion through prayer very regularly everyday. It is not proper even to drink water before prayer, repetition of the Almighty's name, and meditation on him in the heart of hearts.

Rishi-Yajna

Study of scriptures and religious books is called Rishi-Yajna. If it is done, then debts to the sages are paid off. For this reason, every Hindu will have to study the Geeta, Chandi, the Bhagavat, the Puranas, the Upanishads, the Ramayana, the Mahabharata, etc., at his leisure hours to some extent everyday. If anybody fails to read them himself for one reason or the other, he will have to get them read and explained to him by some other person.

Pitri-Yajna

Solemn obsequies performed in honour of the manes of deceased ancestors, the ceremony of offering food and water to them, and similar other rites are known as Pitri-Yajna. If water is presented to the manes of ancestors daily according to prescribed rules and if solemn obsequies are performed monthly or quarterly or annually, then debt to ancestors is paid off. Hence every Hindu has to perform Pitri-Yajna, according to his capacity. Causing satisfaction through devotional service due to the living parents and guardians is also Pitri-Yajna.

Nri-Yajna

Maintenance and rearing of the dependents, charity and service to the blind, invalid, and poor, entertaining guests and helping social welfare work by money and energy are known as Nri-Yajna.

Bhuta-Yajna

Supporting the lower animals (such as—cows, buffaloes, cats, dogs, and such other species) and other living beings—such as plants, creepers, and bushes by food and drink, and rendering service unto them by proper medical aid, constitute Bhuta-Yajna. By such activities debt to living beings is liquidated. It is a daily rite of the Hindus to maintain domestic animals, and serve and rear the plants and trees.

Man has to depend on everything, beginning from the Almighty, downwards to even a negligible straw, for some sort of help, in order to live and continue his existence on the face of the earth. For that reason, every man is more or less indebted to every other form of existence, whether animate or inanimate. As such, all activities throughout the whole span of life ought to be sufficient enough for liquidating the various kinds of debts. No liberation, without liquidation is the principle. Attempts have to be made to liquidate debts by repeated rebirths. The man, who with a full knowledge of everything, attempts, as far as practicable, to liquidate five kinds of debts, by performing five kinds of Yajnas, proceeds speedily towards liberation. For this reason the Hindu saints have prescribed the five kinds of Yajnas for the Hindu society.

TARPANA VIDHI

(The Method of Offering Water)

Every Hindu should offer water at the time of bathing, by taking water in the hollow made by joining the palms together, and reciting the mantras mentioned below:

Tarpana Begins with Deva-tarpana

After bath, standing facing east, in navel-deep water or wearing dry cloth and standing in little depth, water is to be taken in the hollow of the joint palms and then offered, by reciting the following **Mantras**:

ओं ब्रह्मा तृप्यताम् । ओं विष्णुस्तृप्यताम् । ओं रुद्रस्तृप्यताम् ।
ओं प्रजापतिस्तृप्यताम् ।

Oṁ Brahmā tṛpyatām / Oṁ Viṣṇustṛpyatām /
Oṁ Rudrastṛpyatām / Oṁ prajāpatistṛpyatām/[1]

ओं देवा यक्षास्तथा नागा गन्धर्वाप्सरसोऽसुराः ।
क्रूरा सर्पाः सुपर्णाश्च तरवो जिह्मगाः खगाः ।।

Oṁ devāyakṣāstathā nāgā gandharvāpsaraso'surāḥ /
krūrāḥ sarpāḥ suparṇāśca taravo jihmagāḥ khagāḥ //

विद्याधरा जलाधारास्तथैवाकाशगामिनः ।
निराहाराश्च ये जीवा पापे धर्मे रताश्च ये ।
तेषामाप्यायनायैतद् दीयते सलिलं मया ।।

vidyādharā jalādhārāstathaivākāśagāminaḥ /
nirāhārāśca ye jīvā pāpe dharme ratāśca ye /
teṣāmāpyāyanāyaitad dīyate salilaṁ mayā //[2]

Next process is Manushya tarpana
(i.e., Offering water to Original Men)

ओं सनकश्च सनन्दश्च तृतीयश्च सनातनः
कपिलश्चासुरिश्चैव वोढुः पंचशिखस्तथा
सर्वे ते तृप्तिमायान्तु मद्दत्तेनाम्बुना सदा ।

Oṁ sanakaśca sanandaśca tṛtīyaśca sanātanaḥ
kapilaścāsuriścaiva vodhuḥ paṁcaśikhastathā
sarve te tṛptimāyāntu maddattenāmbunā sadā /[3]

---

1. "O Brahma! Be satiated. O Vishnu! Be satiated. O Rudra! Be satiated. O Prajapati! Be satiated."

2. "I have been offering water for the satiety of the Gods, the demi-gods, the serpents, the choristers of heaven, the nymphs of heaven, the demons, the mischievious, the snakes, the sacred birds, the trees, the tortuously moving beings, the birds, the other varieties of demi-gods, the acquatic beings and similarly moving beings of the horizon, the beings which are going without food, those who are vicious, and those who are virtuous."

3. "Let Sanaka, Sanandana, Sanatana, Kapila, Asuri Bardhu and Pancha Shikha be all satisfied with the water offered by me."

Next Process is Rishi Tarpana

ओं मरीचिस्तृप्यताम् । ओं अत्रिस्तृप्यताम् । ओं अंगिरास्तृप्यताम् ।
ओं पुलस्त्यस्तृप्यताम् । ओं पुलहस्तृप्यताम् । ओं क्रतुस्तृप्यताम् ।
ओं प्रचेतास्तृप्यताम् । ओं वसिष्ठस्तृप्यताम् । ओं भृगुस्तृप्यताम् ।
ओं नारदस्तृप्यताम् ।

Oṁ marīcistṛpyatām | Oṁ atristṛpyatām| Oṁ aṅgirāstṛpyatām| Oṁ pulastyastṛpyatām | Oṁ pulahastṛpyatām| Oṁ kratustṛpyatām | Oṁ pracetāstṛpyatām| Oṁ vasiṣṭhastṛpyatām | Oṁ bhṛgustṛpyatām| Oṁ nāradastṛpyatām |[4]

ओं भीष्मः शान्तनवो वीरः सत्यवादी जितेन्द्रियः ।
आभिरद्भिरवाप्नोतु पुत्रपौत्रोचितां क्रियाम् ॥

Oṁ bhīṣmaḥ śāntanavo vīraḥ satyavādī jitendriyaḥ |
ābhiradbhiravāpnotu putrapautrocitām kriyām ||[5]

Next Process is Pitri Tarpana

Later on water is to be offered in due order, by mentioning the name and family name to—father, grand-father, great-grand-father, mother, maternal grand-father, maternal great-grand-father, paternal grand-mother, paternal great-grand-mother, maternal grand-mother, maternal great-grand-mother and others.

Next Process is Rama Tarpana

Water is to be offered by reciting the following mantras:

ओं आब्रह्मभुवनाल्लोका देवर्षिपितृमानवाः ।
तृप्यन्तु पितरः सर्वे मातृमातामहादयाः ॥
अतीतकुलकोटीनाम् सप्तद्वीपनिवासिनाम् ।
मया दत्तेन तोयेन तृप्यन्तु भुवनत्रयम् ॥

---

4. "O Marichi! Be pleased. O Atri! Be pleased. O Angira! Be pleased. O Pulastya! Be pleased. O Pulaha! Be pleased. O Kratu! Be pleased. O Pracheta! Be pleased. O Vashista! Be pleased. O Bhrigu! Be pleased. O Narada! Be pleased."

5. "Let Bhishma, who was the son of Santanu and who was a hero and who was truthful and had full control over the senses, be in peace by this offering of water, usually made by posterity (i.e., by sons and grandsons)."

Oṁ ābrahmabhuvanāllokā devarṣipitṛmānavāḥ /
tṛpyantu pitaraḥ sarve mātṛmātāmahādayāḥ //
atītakulakoṭīnāṁ saptadvīpanivāsinām /
mayā dattena toyena tṛpyantu bhuvanatrayam //[6]

Next Process is Lakshmana Tarpana

Water is to be offered by reciting the following mantra:

ओं आब्रह्मस्तम्बपर्यन्तं जगत् तृप्यतु ।।

Oṁ ābrahmastambaparyantaṁ jagat tṛpyatu/[7]

Finally, Pitri Stuti (i.e., Devotional Prayer to the Ancestors) is to be Recited

ओं पिता स्वर्गः पिता धर्मः पिता हि परमं तपः ।
पितरि प्रीतिमापन्ने प्रीयन्ते सर्वदेवताः ।।

Oṁ pitā svargaḥ pitā dharmaḥ pitā hi paramaṁ tapaḥ /
pitari prītimāpanne prīyante sarvadevatāḥ //[8]

---

6. "Let all the spheres up to Brahma, the absolute, the divine saints, the ancestors and the whole humanity, all my noble ancestors on the paternal and maternal sides, the crores of ancestors of the human race, the residents of the seven continents and also the three worlds be pleased and in peace with the water offered by me."

7. "Let the series of existences beginning with the Brahma the Supreme, be in peace with the water offered by me."

8. "The ancestors are to be regarded as glorious as heaven, as the Dharma, and as the object of supreme penance. They being pleased, all the Gods are propitiated."

SOME QUESTIONS AND ANSWERS ON HINDUISM

Q. 1. Who is the founder of Hindu Dharma?

Ans. Hindu Dharma has no founder, but it is based on the realization of truths and varied experiences of hundreds and thousands of seers in their super-conscious state, from time immemorial. These Divine truths and experiences are collected in the Vedas. So the Vedas are the origin of the Sanatan (the eternal) Hindu Dharma.

Q. 2. Is Hindu Dharma a religion like Islam or Christianity?

Ans. No. Islam or Christianity and other such religions cannot be called Dharma in the true sense of the term. 'Dharma' and 'Religion' are not equivalent words.

Religion consists in accepting some unchangeable and unquestionable doctrines, creeds and dogmas together with a prophet as the inaugurator, a saviour.

Dharma means that which sustains the individual and collective existence of the universe—"ध्रियते अनेन इति धर्मः' '*dhriyate anena iti dharmaḥ*'. Dharma is the universal life-principle and eternal laws by following which material well-being as well as spiritual salvation is attained—"यतोऽभ्युदयनिःश्रेयससिद्धिः स धर्मः" '*yato'bhyudayaniḥśreyasasiddhiḥ sa dharmaḥ*'.

Taken in this sense Hindu Dharma, including its offshoots—Buddhism, Jainism, Zoroastrianism, Sikhism, —can really be called Dharma. Doctrines and creeds there are in Hindu Dharma; but the Hindus know that Dharma does not lie in accepting or rejecting those doctrines and creeds, but essentially in ideals and practice of self-culture. According to Hindu Dharma, every man is potentially Divine; the difference lies in degrees of manifestation. Hindu Dharma with all its paraphernalia aims at gradual unfolding of the Divine in man, by prescribing various rituals and paths of self-culture and domestic and social ideals, duties and responsibilities for people of various status in society, from the highest to the lowest.

Q. 3. With its bewildering variety of doctrines and paths of 'Sadhana', has not Hindu Dharma become a bafflement to its followers as to which path is to be followed?

Ans. Hindu Dharma seems to be a puzzling complexity to the Non-Hindus, the followers of creedal faiths. The complex character of Hindu Dharma is its special feature, wherein lies its greatness. Many men, many minds. No two men in the world are exactly alike in heredities, tastes and capacities. Then how can one expect that certain patent doctrines, creeds, dogmas and rituals should suit all? Is it not like prescribing the same patent medicine for all patients for all sorts of diseases? Prescription and application of the same patent form of religion indiscriminately for all the followers have been responsible for the origin and development of dogmatism and fanaticism in Islam and Christianity.

But Hindu Dharma has determined various paths for various aspirants, according to their needs and tastes and capacities, just like a mother who prepares various kinds of food for her sons—children and adults. Lord Srikrishna declares in the Gita—"Whoever approaches me by whatever path I accept him—"ये यथा मां प्रपद्यन्ते तांस्तथैव भजाम्यहम्" (*ye yathā mām prapadyante tāṁstathaiva bhajāmyaham*'). Hindu scriptures say—"Just as innumerable rivers following various straight or zigzag courses finally merge in the same ocean, so the aspirants of various tastes and capacities following various courses of sadhana ultimately reach Thee—the Supreme.

"रुचीनां वैचित्र्यादृजुकुटिलनानापथजुषाम् ।
नृणामेकगम्यस्त्वमसि पयसामर्णव इव ॥

(*rucīnāṁ vaicitryādṛjukuṭilanānāpathajuṣām* /
nṛṇāmekagamyastvamasi payasāmarṇava iva //)

Herein lies the universal aspect of Hindu Dharma beyond any shade of dogmatism and fanaticism.

Q. 4. Why do the Hindus worship so many gods?

Ans. God has infinite powers and attributes. Each one of the many gods worshipped by the Hindus is the Divine Image of a particular power and attribute of the Lord. So the Hindus do not worship various gods, each independent of another but propitiate various powers and attributes of the Supreme—the One, without a second.

Q. 5. Hindu Dharma preaches Incarnation of God. If God is One, without a second and is the Creator, Preserver and Destructor of the universe then who incarnates?

Ans. Is not God Infinite and Omnipotent? If so, then does not Infinite God minus Infinite God, leave Infinite God?" Shanti path (Peace hymns) "*pūrṇasya pūrṇamādāya pūrṇamevāvaśiṣyate*". "पूर्णस्य पूर्णमादाय पूर्णमेवावशिष्यते" । the Hindu scripture—the Upaniṣad—declares: "Infinity taken from Infinity leaves Infinity".

Q. 6. Islam and Christianity do not admit re-incarnation of human soul and its predestination. Why does Hindu Dharma import it?

Ans. There being no place for rebirth and predestination in Islam and Christianity, they are unable to solve the following two universal questions:

(*a*) Is not God All-merciful? Then why are there in His creation so much of sorrow and misery?

(*b*) Is not God impartial and merciful to all creatures alike? Then why is in the world so much of partiality? Why are some from their very birth rich, meritorious, talented, righteous, healthy, powerful and happy and others poor, stupid, sinful, lame, weak and miserable?

Hindu Dharma has given convincing, rational solutions to these questions through "Janmantara and Karmavada"—"re-incarnation and predestination". Hindu Dharma says—'Every man, nay, every being in the Creation, is potentially God—यत्र जीवस्तत्र शिवः "*yatra jīvas-tatra śivaḥ*". There is no difference between a saint and a sinner except in degree of manifestation. Man is the architect of his own fate and has to enjoy or suffer the results of his good or bad actions. God is the impartial Father of all; He does not make one happy and another miserable. The merits or demerits with which a man is born are results of the good or evil deeds done by him in his past incarnation. Human soul has to be born and re-born again and again to enjoy or suffer the good or bad consequences of his good or evil deeds and to proceed through a long, long process of self-purification till he reaches his journey's end, when he attains perfection and thereby final emancipation.

If re-incarnation of soul and predestination is not admitted then God becomes a merciless despot and an inconsiderate tyrant.

Q. 7. Hindu Dharma, Islam, Christianity—which of these three gives greater freedom to its followers?

Ans. In Hindu Dharma people undoubtedly enjoy the highest freedom because

(*a*) it is essentially a system of self-culture and not bound down by unreasonable creeds and dogmas.

(*b*) It can accommodate even an atheist; for man can proceed in self-culture without admitting God, by simply accepting the ideals and practising the process of self-control and self-discipline.

(*c*) Hindu Dharma prescribes various processes of Sadhana and worship to suit aspirants differing in mentality and belonging to the different strata of society, and never attempts to force all to accept the same patent religious formula. Hence Hindu Dharma alone can accommodate all, rejects none.

(*d*) All followers of Islam are bound to accept Mahomet as the prophet without whose mercy they will have no deliverance; similarly all Christians must accept Christ as the Saviour. But Hindu Dharma has no such binding. A man may be a Hindu without taking shelter in the mercy of any saint or seer, simply if he abides by the instructions and teachings of self-culture of the scriptures.

(*e*) According to Hindu Dharma everyman is potentially Divine and will be able to fully manifest his perfection sooner or later.

Q. 8. What has been the result of this freedom in Hindu Dharma? Are not all dissensions and disruptions in the Hindu society due to this freedom?

Ans. The glorious result of freedom in the practice of Hindu Dharma has been the cause of appearance in the Hindu society, from very ancient times, of thousands of saints and seers, sages, avatars, jnanis, bhaktas and yogis, a negligible fraction of which is not found amongst the followers of other faiths in the world. As regards the dissensions and disruptions prevalent in the Hindu society, they are the baneful effects of a thousand years of foreign domination—political, economic and cultural—that have diverted the Hindus away from their spiritual ideals and practices, and have cast a spell of foreign idealism over their national consciousness and made them indifferent—nay, disdaindul of their own glorious heritage and tradition. In this way the Hindus have almost lost their spiritual background of national unity.

Q. 9. What is the object and meaning of the Arati?

Ans. The Gita, which is the direct message of the Lord incarnated as Sri Srikrishna, and which is universally adored by the Hindus of all classes and creeds, declares that the Supreme is approachable and knowable only through unflagging devotion and complete self-surrender; there is no other path. "भक्त्या मामभि जानाति यावान् यश्चास्मि तत्त्वतः।" "bhaktyā māmabhi jānāti yāvān yaśćāsmi tattvataḥ"—"I am knowable in my real aspect as the Absolute through devotion." सर्वधर्मान् परित्यज्य मामेकं शरणं व्रज" (sarvadharmān parityajya māmekaṁ śaraṇaṁ vraja") "Leave off all rituals and surrender Thyself completely to Me". The Gita confirms that whatever things are offered with devotion to the Lord, He accepts."

पत्रं पुष्पं फलं तोयं यो मे भक्त्या प्रयच्छति।
तदहं भक्त्युपहृतं अश्नामि प्रयतात्मनः॥

"*patraṁ puṣpaṁ phalaṁ toyaṁ yo me bhaktyā prayacchati / tadahaṁ bhaktyupahṛtam aśnāmi prayatātmanaḥ //*"

"If a devotee offers me leaves, flowers, fruits, water, I accept and enjoy those offerings of devotion."

Arati is nothing but the ceremonial offering of love and devotion of one's heart to the Lord through some auspicious symbols and cherished foods. According to the Hindu Shastras the infinite phenomenal world, which is a body of the Infinite, is composed of five fundamental elements—Earth, Water, Fire, Air and Ether. During the Arati-ceremony, we express our love of and devotion to the Lord by offering these five elements symbolically. We offer incense, light, conchshell full of water, fan, music and food.

Incense and food are the symbols of Earth; Conchshell full of water is the symbol of Water, Light is the symbol of Fire, fan is the symbol of Air, Music is the symbol of Ether or Akasha; because sound is produced by vibration in the Ether (Akasha).

Q. 10. Why do the Hindus perform Sraddha ceremony for and offer 'Pindas' to the departed souls of their fore-fathers? Are not these meaningless and useless?

Ans. No. These are neither meaningless nor useless. They have deep spiritual meaning and a definite object.

According to the Hindu scripture (which is supported by modern science also) when a man dies, he leaves off his outer body of flesh and bone but continues to reside in his subtle (astral) body composed of Mind, Senses in subtle form, Intellect and Ego. He has to remain in this state for a period till he is re-born to enjoy or suffer the consequences of his good or evil actions done in his previous birth. So long as he has to reside in the astral body, he suffers untold agony and is relieved by the offerings of love and affection made by his relatives on the earth. Hindu seers saw this by their transcendental vision and made it compulsory for every Hindu to perform sraddha and offer 'Pindas' to their departed fore-fathers. Paying of homage of love and affection to the deceased fore-fathers is observed by the people of other faiths too, only in different forms.

Q. 11. Why do the Hindus worship Hanumana, the Monkey God?

Ans. In Hindu Puranas, Hanumana is regarded as the incarnation of Lord Shiva, the giver of all that is good and beneficial, as well as the destroyer of all evils.

Hanumana is the greatest hero and is known as Mahavira. Hanumana was also the greatest devotee of Lord Rama, the incarnation of the Supreme, and served his master with unflinching devotion and exhibited his supernatural powers and attributes while performing superhuman tasks at the behest of his Lord.

Hence the Hindus worship him ceremoniously to pay their deepest devotion to Mahavira to receive inspirations of undaunted energy and unflinching devotion in the service of the Lord. This is the 'Hindu form of hero worship'.

Q. 12. Why do the Hindus worship ceremoniously the Hanuman-Jhanda (a flag with the murti of Hanumana)? Is it not a superstition?

Ans. Is hoisting of the Union Jack of the English and that of the moon-and-star marked flag of the Mahomedans a superstition? If not, then hoisting of Hanuman-Jhanda after ceremonial worship is also not a superstition.

It has already been said that Mahavira is an incarnation of Lord Shiva and is the embodiment of the highest form of heroism and devotion—Shakti and Bhakti. Hence the national flag of Hindustan, from time immemorial, has been the Hanuman-Jhanda—the emblem of Bhakti and Shakti, of spiritual salvation and material well-being, of energy and heroism, of devotion and service.

Q. 13. God is formless and Impersonal. Why then do the Hindus personify and devise so many forms of God?

Ans. Is not God omnipotent? But if he is Formless only and is unable to assume form, then how can He be attributed to be All-powerful?

This problem has been solved by the realization of the Hindu Seers. They realized God as One Formless, Ultimate Unity, as well as the phenomenal Diversity. Hindu scriptures say that "ekam sad viprā bahudhā vadanti", "God is One but sages realized and named Him as many" "एकं सद् विप्रा बहुधा वदन्ति।" "एकोऽहं बहुस्यां प्रजायेय॥" "Eko'haṁ bahusyāṁ prajāyeya", "I am One, Alone, but I desire to manifest myself as Diversity for enjoyment".

If we apply our common sense, we realize how a man with his limited mind and intellect is incapable of comprehending the Formless One. He can at best meditate on a vast ocean or the blue sky but on nothing formless. If we see through the prayer-forms of the creedal faiths that profess the Formlessness of God, we find that they also unconsciously admit and adore form. Why do the followers of Islam and Christianity turn their faces towards a particular direction during prayer? Why do they hold certain places, things and beings as holy? Why do they pay their homage to and pray for the mercy of the Prophet or the Saviour? Hindu scriptures instruct: "Rtancha satyancha abhidhyat"—one should realize and admit both the Absolute and the phenomenal Unity and Diversity.

Q. 14. Why do the Hindus worship idols?

Ans. No. The Hindus never worship idols but they seek to propitiate God through Divine Images as revealed to the Hindu seers in their deep spiritual trances.

We have already said that God is formless; but at the same time He assumes forms. The Hindu scripture 'Mahānirvāṇa Tantra' says—साधकानां हितार्थाय ब्रह्मणो रूपकल्पना" "sādhakānāṁ hitārthāya brahmaṇo rūpakalpanā"—In order to be easily approachable by the spiritual aspirants, God revealed Himself in Divine Images." So the Images of Hindu gods are not the figments of Imaginative brains but are Divine revelations. Artisans build the Images according to the forms codified by the Hindu scriptures.

Then, again, if anybody listens to the meaning of the 'Mantras', uttered during worship-ceremony of the Hindus, he will at once admit that those mysterious hymns are sung to invoke the grace and benediction of a particular aspect and attribute of God through the Divine Image.

Practical Principles of Hinduism

These principles ought to be observed by every Hindu male and female.

(*A*) *Principles Contributing to Health and Purity*

1. The bed has to be left at Brahmamuhurta, i.e., dawn. The time is one hour prior to the sunrise.

2. Purification by ablution has to be done well, after answering the call of nature. The teeth are to be cleansed and mouth to be washed very regularly.

3. The house, bed, and clothes are to be kept very clean.

4. Food and drink should not be taken any and every time and everywhere indiscriminately.

5. Do not take food without and before prayer, without offering it first to the Almighty and with unwashed mouth; never take the remains of another's meal. There is no objection to taking the remains of the food offered to God or taken by Gurudeva or by one's parents.

6. One should not be addicted to intoxicants, such as, cannabis, wine, opium, etc. and should gradually try to give up the habit of taking tea, smoking cigarettes, cigar, tobacco, etc.

7. One should give up idle games, such as playing cards and chess, playing at dice, etc.; in lieu of which one should take to physical culture, such as outdoor games or exercises, or a laborious work.

8. Hindus' forbidden food, such as egg, fish, meat, onion, garlic, etc. should not be taken.

(*B*) *Principles Contributing to Physical Restraint*

1. One should control and regulate one's passions and senses.

2. Young boys should control and preserve semen very carefully instead of dissipating it.

3. Married people also should practise control over the senses.

4. One should not take such food as excites the senses.

Practical directions and means of retaining semen and observing Brahmacharya have been elaborately discussed in AUM BRAHMACHARYAM published by our Sangha.

The duties and responsibilities of an ideal householder have been discussed in AUM GARHASTYAM.

(*C*) *Principles Contributing to Mental Restraint*

1. One should always remain engaged in some useful work.

2. One should read the Ramayana, the Mahabharata, the Puranas, the Geeta, the Bhagavat, the Upanishads, or some other instructive literature either alone or in company, during spare time. It is advisable not to go through trashy dramas and novels and watch demoralising talkies and cinema shows.

3. If anybody happens to commit a sin or be engaged in vicious thought in a weak moment, he will have to take the vow of not repeating the same thing again, after expiating the sin by apologizing to the Almighty and repeating the Divine name with a repentant heart.

4. One should be in Divine communion through prayer every dawn and dusk.

(D) Principles Regarding Family Life

1. One should revere and respect one's parents and superiors and serve them with whole-hearted devotion.

2. The members of the same family, young and old alike, should maintain a common bond of love and affection, regard and reverence. Mutual faults and shortcomings should not be taken into consideration at all.

3. As far as practicable, all the members of a family should be in Divine communion through joint prayer, and should also pray to the Almighty for the welfare of the Hindu society as a whole.

4. During spare time the guardians will sit with all the other members of the family together and read and discuss the Ramayana, the Mahabharata, etc.

5. The guardian will assign the family duties and responsibilities to its members according to their ability and fitness.

6. Every individual member of a family will think of the welfare and prosperity of the whole family and make whatever efforts he can for their attainment.

7. Selfishness should be condemned as a great vice.

8. Individual pleasure and interest must be sacrificed for the good of the entire family.

(E) Principles Regarding Social Life

1. The Hindus of all castes and creeds, whatever their status and circumstance, should mix as brothers and co-operate with one another in every possible way.

2. Those capable of helping others should render whatever help they can to those Hindu brethren who are helpless, miserable and impecunious.

3. The educated and ritualistic Hindus should not neglect and hate those who are uneducated and depressed in their society. On the contrary, they should arrange to educate them in morality, religion, health and rituals, with a view to making them educated and trained in right conduct.

4. He who will take up any work for the good of the Hindu society and nationality should be taken care of and helped in every possible way by all other Hindu brothers.

5. Hindus should offer mass-prayer on special ceremonial occasions.

6. They should live in an organised way, united by a bond of mutual intimacy and fellow-feeling and should also organise joint defence in the face of any danger or difficulty.

7. Personal and family interests and comforts must be sacrificed for the good of the society.

BASIC PRINCIPLES OF HINDUISM

1. Everyone should have unflinching faith and confidence in the Almighty and in religion.

2. Everyone should be faithful and devoted to Guru (preceptor), saints, and religion.

3. One should follow the Hindu code of morals and right conduct.

4. One should be attached to one's own religion and follow the rituals.

5. The Hindu style and standard must be maintained, as far as practicable, in food, in dress and in habit.

6. One must be in Divine communion through prayer every day.

7. He must take to physical culture in order to develop prowess and strength.

8. He must practise the method of doing organised work.

9. He must be proud of Hinduism, Hindu Dharma, Hindu society, culture and civilization.

10. He must organise the Hindus and infuse a spirit of co-operation in them with a view to repulsing the attacks upon Hindu religion and defending the Hindu society from various onslaughts.

THE SHIVA PUJA

(ABRIDGED SYSTEM OF WORSHIP OF THE LORD SHIVA SUITED TO ALL)

Lord Shiva is to be worshipped in a *Shiva Lingam* made of earth, stone or metal; the Shiva-Lingam made of earth should be prepared readily at the time of worship and thrown into the water after the ceremony is finished. The Shiva-Lingam made of earth ought to be of the size of the thumb (i.e., two inches) in length and circumference; it should be placed on a bel-leaf or on a stone-plate or a metal plate, where bel-leaf is not available. '*Lingam*' means an emblem. '*Shiva-Lingam*' means an emblem of Shiva, through which *Lord Shiva* is worshipped and propitiated.

Jalashuddhi

(Purification of water)

Water is to be taken in a brass or copper vessel and should be purified with the Mantras mentioned in the foregoing chapter on the "Procedure of Sandhya-Vandana".

Achmana

(Purification of the body and sense-organs)

Next, purification of the body and sense-organs should be performed with the touch of the fingers, wetted in water, uttering the mantras given in the chapter on the 'Procedure of Sandhya-Vandana,' under the heading "*Achmana*" and "*Indriya-Sparsha.*"

Dhyanam

Next, with a flower in the palm, meditation and concentration of mind on Lord Shiva is to be done uttering the following mantra.

ॐ ध्यायेन्नित्यं महेशं रजतगिरिनिभं चारुचन्द्रावतंसम् ।
पद्मासीनं समन्तात् स्तुतममरगणैर्व्याघ्रकृत्तिं वसानम् ।।
विश्वाद्यं विश्ववीजं निखिलभयहरं पंचवक्त्रं त्रिनेत्रम् ।
नानालंकारदीप्तं स्फटिकमणिप्रभं धूर्जटीं पार्वतीशम् ।।

Oṁ dhyāyennityaṁ maheśaṁ rajatagirinibhaṁ cārucandrā-vataṁsam/ padmāsīnaṁ samantāt stutamamaragaṇairvyā-ghrakṛttiṁ vasānam// viśvādyaṁ viśva-vījaṁ nikhilabhaya-haraṁ pañcavaktraṁ trinetram/ nānālaṅkāradīptaṁ sphaṭi-kamaṇiprabhaṁ dhūrjaṭīṁ pārvatīśaṁ//[1]

With the above meditation completed, the flower should be put on the centre of the roof of the head and mental worship is to be performed for a few minutes.

Then with joined palms *Lord Shiva* is to be invited to appear in the *Lingam* and accept the offerings of devotion:

"ॐ पिनाकधृक् इहागच्छ, इहागच्छ, इह तिष्ठ, इह तिष्ठ, इह सन्निधेहि, इह सन्निरुद्धस्व, अत्राधिष्ठानं कुरु, मम पूजां गृहाण।"

"*Oṁ pinākadhṛk ihāgaccha, ihāgaccha, iha tiṣṭha, iha tiṣṭha, iha sannidhehi, iha sanniruddhasva, atrādhiṣṭhānaṁ kuru, mama pujāṁ gṛhāṇa/*"[2]

Then *Lord Shiva* in the Lingam is to be bathed with curd, milk, clarified butter, honey and sugar mixed together and then with water (where these things are not available, only with water), uttering the mantra—ॐ पशुपतये नमः "*Oṁ paśupataye namaḥ.*"

Then the *Lingam* is to be smeared with sandal-paste with the mantraṁ ॐ महेश्वराय नमः "*Oṁ maheśvarāya namaḥ.*"

Then after meditation for the second time as before, *Lord Shiva* is to be worshipped and propitiated with offerings of flowers, smeared with sandal-paste successively uttering the following Mantras:—

1. I meditate devotionally upon *Lord Shiva* who shines like a mountain of silver, who has the moon-cresent on His fore-head; who is seated on a full-blown lotus; who has worn a piece of tiger-skin round His waist and who is being propitiated and encircled by the gods; who is the origin and seed of the universe; who is the dispeller of all sorts of fears; who has five mouths and three eyes; who is adorned with various jewels, shining like precious crystal; who is named Dhurjati and Lord of Parvati, the mother of the universe (i.e. the primal Energy.)

2. "O holder of the dreadful bow *Piṇāka,* come here please, stay here, appear before me, take your seat steadily in this *Lingam* and accept my devotional offerings."

एते गन्धपुष्पे ॐ सर्वाय क्षितिमूर्तये नमः ।
एते गन्धपुष्पे ॐ भवाय जलमूर्तये नमः ।
एते गन्धपुष्पे ॐ रुद्राय अग्निमूर्तये नमः ।
एते गन्धपुष्पे ॐ उग्राय वायुमूर्तये नमः ।
एते गन्धपुष्पे ॐ भीमाय आकाशमूर्तये नमः ।
एते गन्धपुष्पे ॐ महादेवाय सोममूर्तये नमः ।
एते गन्धपुष्पे ॐ पशुपतये यजमानमूर्तये नमः ।
एते गन्धपुष्पे ॐ ईशानाय सूर्यमूर्तये नमः ।

ete gandha-puṣpe oṁ sarvāya kṣitimūrtaye namaḥ/
ete gandha-puṣpe oṁ bhavāya jalamūrtaye namaḥ/
ete gandha-puṣpe oṁ rudrāya agnimūrtaye namaḥ/
ete gandha-puṣpe oṁ ugrāya vāyumūrtaye namaḥ/
ete gandha-puṣpe oṁ bhīmāya ākāśamūrtaye namaḥ/
ete gandha-puṣpe oṁ mahādevāya somamūrtaye namaḥ/
ete gandha-puṣpe oṁ paśupataye yajamānamūrtaye namaḥ/
ete gandha-puṣpe oṁ īśānāya sūryamūrtaye namaḥ/[3]

Then comes "Japam" or repetition of the Mantram.

ॐ गुरु नमः शिवाय—"*Oṁ guru namaḥ śivāya*" this mantra is to be repeated at least one hundred and eight times. Then self-dedication to the feet of Lord Shiva is to be made uttering the following mantra:—

---

3. With this offering of flowers and sandal-paste, I worship and bow down to *Sarva* in the form of the Earth;

With this offering of flowers and sandal-paste, I worship and bow down to *Bhava* in the form of Water;

With this offering of flowers and sandal-paste, I worship and bow down to *Rudra* in the form of Fire;

With this offering of flowers and sandal-paste, I worship and bow down to *Ugra* in the form of Air;

With this offering of flowers and sandal-paste, I worship and bow down to *Bhima* in the form of the Sky;

With this offering of flowers and sandal-paste, I worship and bow down to *Mahādeva* in the form of the Moon;

With this offering of flowers and sandal-paste, I worship and bow down to *Paśupati* in the form of the animate universe;

With this offering of flowers and sandal-paste, I worship and bow down to *Īśāna* in the form of the Sun.

"*Sarva*", "*Bhava*", "*Rudra*", "*Ugra*", "*Bhīma*", "*Maheśvara*", "*Paśupati*" and "*Īśāna*" are the eight significant names of *Lord Shiva*; the Earth, the Sun, the Moon, the Water, the Air, the Fire, the Sky, the animate universe are all pervaded by the infinite Spiritual Existence of Lord Shiva.

गुह्यातिगुह्य गोप्ता त्वं गृहाणास्मत्कृतं जपम् ।
सिद्धिर्भवतु मे देव त्वत्प्रसादात् सुरेश्वर ॥

Oṁ guhyātiguhya goptā tvaṁ gṛhāṇāsmatkṛtam japam |
siddhirbhavatu me deva tvatprasādāt sureśvara ||

"Thou art unknown and unknowable, please accept our worship and be propitiated; may I attain emancipation by Thy grace."

Then one should bow down to Lord Shiva, uttering the following mantras:—

ॐ नमस्तुभ्यं विरूपाक्षं नमस्ते दिव्यचक्षुषे ।
नमः पिनाकहस्ताय वज्रहस्ताय वै नमः ॥

Oṁ namastubhyaṁ virūpākṣṁ namaste divyacakṣuṣe |
namaḥ pinākahastāya vajrahastāya vai namaḥ ||[4]

नमस्त्रिशूलहस्ताय दण्डपाशासिपाणये ।
नमस्त्रैलोक्यनाथाय भूतानां पतये नमः ॥

namastriśūlahastāya daṇḍapāśāsipāṇaye |
namastrailokyanāthāya bhūtānaṁ pataye namaḥ ||[5]

नमः शिवाय शान्ताय कारणत्रयहेतवे ।
निवेदयामि चात्मानं त्वं गतिः परमेश्वर ॥

namaḥ śivāya śāntāya kāraṇatrayahetave |
nivedayāmi cātmānaṁ tvaṁ gatiḥ parameśvara ||[6]

ŚIVĀṢṬAKAM
(HYMNS TO SHIVA)

प्रभुमीशमनीशमशेषगुणं, गुणहीनमहीशगराभरणम् ।
रणनिर्जितदुर्जयदैत्यपुरं, प्रणमामि शिवं शिवकल्पतरुम् ॥

4. I bow down with profound devotion to Virūpākṣa who has Divine eye-sight, who has the dreadful bow and also vajra in His hands.

5. I bow down devotionally to Lord Shiva who has Trident and Daṇḍa, pāśā and sword in His hands, who is the Lord of the three worlds and who is the ruler of the five original elements of creation.

6. I bow down devotionally to Lord Shiva who is calm and serene, who is the cause of creation, protection and destruction, I resign myself to Thee. Thou art the only refuge of mine.

prabhumīśamanīśamaśeṣaguṇaṁ
guṇahīnamahīśagarābharaṇam/
raṇanirjitadurjayadaityapuraṁ
praṇamāmi śivam śivakalpatarum //[1]

गिरिराजसुतान्वितवामतनुं, तनुनिन्दितराजितकोटिविधुम् ।
विधिविष्णुशिरस्तुतपादयुगं, प्रणमामि शिवं शिवकल्पतरुम् ।।

girirājasutānvitavāmatanuṁ
tanuninditarājitakoṭividhum/
vidhiviṣṇuśirastutapādayugaṁ
praṇamāmi śivaṁ śivakalpatarum//[2]

शशलांछितरंजितसन्मुकुटं, कटिलम्बित-सुन्दर-कृत्तिपटम् ।
सुरशैवलिनीकृतपूतजटं, प्रणमामि शिवं शिवकल्पतरुम् ।।

śaśalāñchitaraṁjitasanmukuṭaṁ
kaṭilambita-sundara-kṛttipaṭam/
suraśaivalinīkṛtapūtajaṭaṁ
praṇamāmi śivaṁ śivakalpatarum //[3]

नयनत्रयभूषितचारुमुखं, मुखपद्मपराजितकोटिविधुम् ।
विधुखण्ड-विमण्डित-भालतटं, प्रणमामि शिवं शिवकल्पतरुम् ।।

nayanatrayabhūṣitacārumukhaṁ
mukhapadmaparājitakoṭividhum /
vidhukhaṇḍa-vimaṇḍita-bhālataṭam
praṇamāmi śivaṁ śivakalpatarum //[4]

---

1. O Shiva! Thou art the Lord-Absolute and the Governor of the Universe, the abode of infinite glory, adorned with the garland of the princes of snakes. (Snakes are the emblems of Śakti, according to Hindu scriptures). Thou didst kill the great demon Pura; I bow down to Thee, the Kalpataru, that fulfils one's heart's desire.

2. O Shiva! The daughter of the mountain king, the mother of the universe, is the left half of Thy body; the body is shining white as if with the rays of a million moons; Thy feet is adored by the creator and protector of the universe; I bow down to Thee, the fulfiller of all desires.

3. O Shiva! The crown on Thy head surpasses even the moon with its beauteous effulgence; Thou hast worn a beautiful tiger-skin round Thy waist; Thy matted locks of hair have been sanctified by the divine river current of the Ganga; I bow down to Thee, the fulfiller of all prayers.

4. O Shiva! The beautiful face glows with three eyes; Thy lotus-face defeats a million moons in serene beauty; Thy forehead is shining with a digit of the moon; I bow down to Thee, the dispenser of desired objects.

वृषराजनिकेतनमादिगुरुं, गरलाशनमाजिविषाणधरम् ।
प्रमथाधिपसेवकरंजनकं, प्रणमामि शिवं शिवकल्पतरुम् ॥

vṛṣarājaniketanamādigurum̐
garalāśanamājiviṣāṇadharam /
pramathādhipasevakaram̐janakam̐
praṇamāmi śivam̐ śivakalpatarum //[5]

मकरध्वजमत्तमातंगहरं, करिचर्मसनाथविबोधकरम् ।
वराभयशूलविषाणधरं, प्रणमामि शिवं शिवकल्पतरुम् ॥

makaradhvajamattamātam̐gaharam̐
karicarmasanāthavibodhakaram /
varābhayaśūlaviṣāṇadharam̐
praṇamāmi śivam̐ śivakalpatarum//[6]

जगदुद्भवपालननाशकरं, कृपयैक पुनस्त्रयरूपधरम् ।
प्रियमानवसाधुजनैकगतिं, प्रणमामि शिवं शिवकल्पतरुम् ॥

jagadudbhavapālananāśakaram̐
kṛpayaika punastrayarūpadharam /
priyamānavasādhujanaikagatim̐
praṇamāmi śivam̐ śivakalpatarum //[7]

महेशविश्वेशविश्वविभो, पुनर्जन्मदुःखात् परित्राहि शम्भो ।
भजतोऽखिलदुःखसमूहहरं, प्रणमामि शिवं शिवकल्पतरुम् ॥

maheśaviśveśaviśvavibho
punarjanmaduḥkhāt paritrāhi śambho /
bhajato'khiladuḥkhasamūhaharam̐
praṇamāmi śivam̐ śivakalpatarum //[8]

---

5. O Shiva! Thou ridest on the back of a divine bullock, Thou art the only saviour; Thou drank the venom that threatened the world with extinction; Thou carriest the divine bugle; Thou art the Lord of the Pramathas and lover of the devotees; I bow down to Thee, the desire-tree.

6. O Shiva! Thou art the destroyer of Cupid, the veritable wild elephant; Thou art the giver of protection and [granter of] prayers; Thou hast the trident and Viṣāṇa in Thy hands; I bow down to Thee, the giver of all desired objects.

7. O Shiva! Thou art the creator, protector and destroyer of the universe; Thou art one; but still kindly assumest three different forms; Thou art the only refuge of the pious mankind; I bow down to Thee, the vouchsafer of all desires.

8. O Shiva! Thou art the Lord of Lords; Thou art the Lord of the Cosmos; Thou art the cosmic powers; save me from the miseries of recurrent births and deaths and kindly allay the sufferings of Thy devotees; I bow down to Thee, the granter of all hearts' desires.